The Teacher's Toolbox For Every Child

Activities to Build Children's Strengths Through Art, Improv and Conversation

Peggy Stern and **Diana Baron-Moore**

Copyright © 2024 by SuperDvilleLLC

For further information go to SuperDville.com

For inquiries, please write questions@superdville.com

Published by McCoral Publishing,

Oaks, PA

All rights reserved. No part of this publication may be reproduced, stored in a retrieval system, or transmitted, in any form or by any means, electronic, mechanical, photocopying, recording, or otherwise, without the prior permission of the publishers.

Table of Contents

From the Authors 4
How to Use This Book 6
Credits and Acknowledgements 8

Identifying Emotions 9
Discussion Guide 10
Read Aloud: Ping Pong Pressure 11
SEL Vocabulary 12
Activity 1: The Mirror Game 13
Activity 2: What Flavors Are Your Feelings? 14
Activity 3: School Feelings 18
Activity 4: Illustrating Feelings 20
Extension Activity 1: Double Scoop Coloring Sheet ... 21
Extension Activity 2: What Does a Feeling Look Like? Guessing Game 21

Stress 23
Discussion Guide 24
Read Aloud: Stress Mess 25
SEL Vocabulary 26
Activity 1: Stressed Body / Calm Body 27
Activity 2: De-stressing Strategy Bank 28
Activity 3: Best Fit Strategy 31
Activity 4: What I Can and Can't Control 33
Extension Activity 1: Stressed Body / Calm Body ... 35
Extension Activity 2: De-stressing Dance Party ... 35

Perseverance 37
Discussion Guide 38
Read Aloud: Never Give Up 39
SEL Vocabulary 40
Activity 1: Perseverance Comic 41
Activity 2: Perseverance Role Play 43
Activity 3: Goal Setting 45
Activity 4: An Inspiring Thought 48
Extension Activity 1: What Happens Next? 50
Extension Activity 2: Working Toward My Goal 50

Gratitude 53
Discussion Guide 54
Read Aloud: Lost in the Park 55
SEL Vocabulary 56
Activity 1: Thank You Card 57
Activity 2: Silver Lining Craft Project 59
Activity 3: The Best Part of My Day 60
Activity 4: A Kind Place 61
Extension Activity 1: Gratitude Wall 63

Extension Activity 2: Thank You Card Design Challenge 63

Curiosity 65
Discussion Guide 66
Read Aloud: The Mess-O-Matic 3000 67
SEL Vocabulary 69
Activity 1: Active Listening Game 70
Activity 2: Design It Your Way 72
Activity 3: Self-Discovery Writing 73
Activity 4: Research Scavenger Hunt 74
Extension Activity 1: Self-Discovery Poem 76
Extension Activity 2: Create a New Class 76

Self-Acceptance 77
Discussion Guide 78
Read Aloud: Professor Boom and the Dyslexic Brain .. 79
SEL Vocabulary 80
Activity 1: Self-Love Self-Portrait 81
Activity 2: Affirmation Mirror 82
Activity 3: Every Side of Me Accordion Book 83
Activity 4: Every Brain Is Different 85
Extension Activity 1: Mirror Talk 3 by 3 88
Extension Activity 2: Journal Prompt 88

Confidence 89
Discussion Guide 90
Read Aloud: Confidence Hat 91
SEL Vocabulary 92
Activity 1: Strengths Bingo 93
Activity 2: Best Friend Voice 96
Activity 3: Comfort Zone Challenge 98
Activity 4: Listening Circle 100
Extension Activity 1: Create Your Own Strengths Bingo Card 101
Extension Activity 2: Stretch Zone Challenge ... 101

Self-Advocacy 103
Discussion Guide 104
Read Aloud: Resource Room 105
SEL Vocabulary 106
Activity 1: Self-Advocacy Role Play 107
Activity 2: Megaphone Activity 110
Activity 3: Your Perfect Learning Space 113
Activity 4: Super D! Letters 114
Extension Activity 1: Dear Teacher 118
Extension Activity 2: Self-Advocacy Comic Strip ... 118

From the Authors

Dear Reader,

I am so glad you have chosen *The Teacher's Toolbox For Every Child*!

When I was diagnosed with dyslexia as a child, no one talked about learning differences. I thought I was the only one who struggled with reading. A few days a week after school, I would head to Mrs. Pace, a trained Orton Gillingham reading teacher. I was lucky to have someone in my life who helped me feel less frustrated and alone. Though she did eventually teach me how to read, her most important lesson was in helping me to discover and have confidence in my strength: storytelling.

Mrs. Pace would not only type up the stories I dictated to her, but she would also use them as the basis for our lessons! My self-esteem soared, and I embarked on a life of storytelling that has led me to a career in film, an Academy Award, and now, the video-based SuperDville curriculum that serves as the inspiration and source material for this book.

The "strength-based model" that Mrs. Pace so successfully used focuses on a core truth that we at SuperDville take seriously: encourage your students to find, explore, and celebrate the things they enjoy, and they will shine.

This book is an extension of SuperDville, an SEL curriculum for kids with learning disabilities (or differences, as we call them). SuperDville is a video-based SEL program with curricula and hands-on activities for kids with dyslexia, dyscalculia, dysgraphia, and ADHD. The program empowers LD kids by giving them strategies to cope with issues related to self-esteem, resilience, perseverance, self-advocacy, empathy, and belonging.

Though we created SuperDville with kids with learning differences in mind, we've been thrilled to learn that teachers use it in general education classrooms, as the themes resonate with **ALL** children.

> The read-alouds that introduce each chapter are adapted from SuperDville videos written by myself and two other dyslexic filmmakers, David Bailen and Max Streble. We also worked with child development experts and educators to ensure that our scripts and accompanying curriculum aligned with the themes selected by the gold standard in Social Emotional Learning: The Council on Academic Social and Emotional Learning (CASEL).

The response to SuperDville from educators and students has been exceptional and we felt it was important to extend the web experience offline by creating *The Teacher's Toolbox for Every Child* curriculum, co-written by gifted educator and SuperDville Educational Content Developer, Diana Baron-Moore. With this book, Diana has created a rich, creative, and effective SEL curriculum that **all** children can benefit from.

I would love you to explore SuperDville.com, and encourage you to sign up for our newsletter to learn about future offers, discounts, and our subscriber's Facebook page.

Thank you for inviting us into your classroom and for taking the steps to inspire kids as Mrs. Pace inspired me, by helping them discover their strengths and making them know that they are not alone.

Peggy Stern

Dear Reader,

Thank you for picking up this book. It has been a true pleasure to contribute to this collection of stories and activities. I hope that you will find resources in these pages that bring out your students' creativity, critical thinking, and sense of community as they build the skills and capacities they need to take ownership of their learning.

I came to this project following several years of running arts and play programming for children with disabilities at a non-profit in Brooklyn, NY. My experiences in the art room and sensory gym were a practice ground for the approaches embedded in the activities here: open-ended prompts, centering students' emotional experiences in real-time, and connecting through play.

My connection to this work is personal—grown from my own experiences as an unidentified neurodivergent child as well as from my love for the kids who have a hard time fitting themselves into the structures and expectations of the classroom. I know about the ways that feeling worry, shame, and exclusion at school can interrupt learning. I wish deeply that I had had an adult intent on helping me to understand my needs and emotions during the intense years of upper elementary school.

That is why I am so delighted that you will be offering social emotional learning support to your students! It is my sincere hope that this book will offer you many opportunities to affirm and connect with them while also being of genuine use as they navigate life at school. Meeting students as full people requires a tremendous amount of energy, patience, and skill. Thank you for your generosity in giving this to your students.

With gratitude,

Diana Baron-Moore

How to Use This Book

What is the goal of this book?

This curriculum aims to teach attitudes and habits of mind that sustain students' positive self-concept as they face academic challenges, develop a growing awareness of their neurological differences, and navigate increasingly complex social dynamics. These lessons are not about study strategies or prescriptive social rules. The exploratory nature of these activities will help you introduce important conversations about self-worth, resilience, and community.

This book is built around eight stories about *The Super D! Kids*, characters with learning differences from the social and emotional learning (SEL) web series on SuperDville.com. The read-alouds in the chapters trace a thematic journey through skills and traits students need to develop as they take agency over their learning and growth. Students will begin by deepening their emotional literacy. Then, they will develop strategies for meeting the challenges of stress and perseverance. Next, they will find resources in their curiosity, learn about the value of gratitude, and cultivate self-acceptance and confidence. Finally, they will practice self-advocacy.

The activities in this book will prompt kids to self-reflect and communicate with one another about their inner lives using art, play, and discussion. The read-alouds will help you open the door to fruitful conversations about students' inner lives. The lessons include many open-ended, art-based explorations paired with targeted discussion questions to get kids thinking deeply.

What's included?

- ✓ 8 read-alouds based on episodes from the SuperDville! online curriculum with accompanying vocabulary lists, discussion guides, and audio versions available online
- ✓ 32 activities that leverage art, play, and conversation with print and downloadable PDF versions of all accompanying worksheets
- ✓ 16 extension activities to offer early finishers and students who want a challenge
- ✓ Exclusive digital coloring sheets available online

Who is this book for?

The stories and activities in this book are designed for students in upper elementary, but can also be enjoyed by younger or older kids. These themes, while often particular pain points for children with learning differences, will be familiar to all children and offer a rich space in which to explore social and emotional skills–finding the confidence to try new things, persevering through challenges, navigating tricky emotions, and more.

As educators, you know your students best! Teachers may find this lens of the book particularly useful in their work of building a culture of openness in which learning differences are destigmatized and welcomed. Parents, tutors, and other school staff may also find these activities supportive of their goals.

Classroom Practices

As you make these activities your own, the following guiding principles will support positive experiences for your students. It will be important to keep a few things in mind:

 A key goal of this book is to lead students toward the development of flexible self-advocacy strategies. The more that students feel agency over their own learning, the more that their intrinsic motivation will kick in. Encourage students' creative responses as deep expressions of their capacity to problem solve.

 When students share about their challenges, it is important to validate their experiences and emotions. Before offering strategies and solutions, it is often helpful to pause and listen. Demonstrating curiosity and interest goes a long way when students are struggling.

 Since SEL can be a sensitive topic, we encourage you to collaborate with your team when needed. Other teachers, support staff, and mental health professionals are valuable resources to call on.

Modifications

We encourage you to make these activities just right for your students. Below are some ideas about adjusting these lessons for various settings and a few guidelines we recommend following, regardless of the modifications you make.

- Follow the activities in order, or select lessons as the themes arise organically throughout the year.

- Lessons are designed for groups, however, a majority of them can be adjusted to use with individual students.

- When working with younger students, it is appropriate to break lessons into two days. Many lessons include a discussion or brainstorming as the hook. These anticipatory activities can be delivered on a separate day.

- If older students show interest in deeper exploration, you may expand on the closure discussion by adding a partner share component or building on the extension activities.

We hope you enjoy using this book and would love to hear ideas that emerge as you explore it further!

We invite you to join the Teacher's Toolbox Facebook group where you can connect with other teachers, share resources, and compare notes with other dedicated professionals in the field.

For more information and to access the digital resources, please visit SuperDville.com.

The Teacher's Toolbox For Every Child

Credits and Acknowledgements

Credits:

A Book By: Peggy Stern and Diana Baron-Moore

Designer: Jessica Trippe

Illustrations: Jiaxin Ying, Áine Gleeson

Original SuperDville Scripts: David Bailen, Peggy Stern, and Max Strebel

Audio of Stories: Ashika Shah and Andres Correa

Acknowledgments:

Everyone at SuperDville.com contributed to this book by working with enthusiastic commitment to our mission and ensuring our content is creative and impactful for kids. We would especially like to thank Diana Correa-Cintron for her enduring optimism and Ashika Shah for being her multi-talented self. Dr. Sherryl Graves, thank you for editing the book to meet proper standards of diversity, equity, and inclusion. The stories and curriculum were significantly enhanced by the additional writing contributions of Adrienne Vrettos. Thank you to Cigdem Knebel, who envisioned this book before anyone else and who has gone way beyond the efforts of a traditional publisher sharing her editing skills and content ideas all along the way. Dondi Tondro-Smith, your content editing added so much and Michelle Levy, you added extra wisdom along with your copy editing. Jiaxin Ying, you floored us all with your charming and whimsical illustrations and we could not be more grateful for the life they brought to the book. Áine Gleeson you jumped in at the end and created wonderful illustrations as if you had been with us since day one. Jessica Trippe, with your illuminating talents as a designer, you took a black and white book and infused it with fun and style. Lastly, thank you to all the neurodiverse children who have been our teachers–it is a true joy to learn and grow alongside you.

Chapter 1:
Identifying Emotions

Discussion Guide

READ ALOUD OBJECTIVE
In this chapter, students will explore identifying emotions. By naming their emotions in fictional situations, observing and identifying the feelings of others, and considering how their emotions can be complex, students will develop skills and vocabulary that will increase their understanding of themselves and others. Specifically, students will explore how they feel about their school day and identify how each part of their day makes them feel.

STORY SUMMARY
When Kaylee and Logan hear a strange noise in the rec room, they discover their friend Matias is playing ping-pong… in the dark! Soon, Rowan and Elsworth join Kaylee and Logan in watching Matias, who impresses them all with his ping-pong skills. When his friends start gushing to Matias about how great he is and ask about his plans to compete in tournaments, Matias sneaks away. When Logan finds him, Matias shares that playing alone makes him feel calm and happy, and playing in front of a crowd makes him feel stressed. After sharing his feelings with Logan, Matias is able to tell his friends how he feels about playing ping-pong.

COMPREHENSION QUESTIONS

1. **Why was Matias playing ping-pong with a headlamp on?**
   Answer: He likes to play in the dark to help himself feel calm.

2. **Why did Matias leave when his friends said nice things about his ping-pong skills?**
   Answer: Matias didn't like feeling his friends' expectations about being good at ping-pong and competing.

3. **Where did Logan find Matias?**
   Answer: Logan found Matias in the storage closet.

READ ALOUD INTRODUCTION
Today, we will read a story about a boy named Matias. He loves to play ping-pong, but only when no one is watching. Let's read the story and see if we can determine why.

READ ALOUD CLOSURE
Identifying and naming our feelings is an important skill. Being mindful of our emotions helps us enjoy our good feelings and find ways to cope when we are stressed or sad. Matias found that playing ping-pong made him feel calm and happy. We can find our own strategies that help us recognize and cope with our emotions.

DISCUSSION QUESTIONS

1. What do you think Logan meant when she said the kids broke Matias's calm bubble?

2. Why did Matias rush out of the room where he was playing when his friends came in?

3. Do you have any special activities you do to calm down when you are frustrated?

LISTEN TO THE AUDIO VERSION OF THE STORY

READ ALOUD:
Ping Pong Pressure

"Do you hear that?" Kaylee asks as she and Logan open the door to the rec room.

Logan listens, peering into the dark room. *Ponk! Ponk! Ponk!* A sound is coming from inside.

"Turn on the lights!" Logan whispers. "It might be a mouse!"

Kaylee flicks on the light, and the kids blink at the scene before them.

"Does your mouse play ping-pong?" Kaylee asks.

Half of the ping-pong table is raised up, making it the perfect backboard for Matias, who is hitting a ping-pong ball with his paddle in the dark while wearing a headlamp flashlight on his forehead.

"Hey guys," Matias says, switching off the headlamp and continuing to hit the ball without missing a beat.

"Matias!" Logan says, rushing over to get a closer look. "You're amazing!"

"I'm pretty good, I guess," Matias shrugs.

"*Pretty* good?" Kaylee scoffs, joining Logan to watch.

"You're GREAT!" shouts a voice from the doorway as Elsworth hurries over to Matias.

"I bet you could crush everyone in a ping-pong tournament," he says, sounding like a commentator.

Matias catches the ping-pong ball and stuffs it with his paddle into his sweatshirt pocket. With a shrug, he takes a step back.

"But why were you playing in the dark?" Kaylee asks as Matias moves toward the door. "Is that part of your training?"

Matias hurries out of the room.

"Want us to turn the lights back off?" Elsworth calls after him.

The friends gathered around the ping-pong table look at each other in confusion. "That was weird," Logan says.

"Yeah," Kaylee agrees. "If I were that good at ping-pong, I'd want everyone to see."

"Where do you think he went?" Elsworth asks.

"I think I know," Logan says. "Leave it to me."

A few moments later, Logan knocks on a door marked STORAGE CLOSET in the hallway. "Matias? You in there?"

There is no answer, but just a soft sound. *Pock! Pock! Pock!*

continued next page

Chapter 1 Activities

Activity 1: **The Mirror Game**
Activity Type: Game

Activity 2: **What Flavors Are Your Feelings?**
Activity Type: Craft

Activity 3: **School Feelings**
Activity Type: Worksheet

Activity 4: **Illustrating Feelings**
Activity Type: Art

Extension 1: **Double Scoop Coloring Sheet**
Activity Type: Worksheet

Extension 2: **What Does a Feeling Look Like? Guessing Game**
Activity Type: Game

SEL Vocabulary

emotion [noun]: a mood or state of mind that changes in response to what is happening around us

feeling [noun]: an emotion or a sensation in our body

happy [adjective]: an emotion that people feel when something happens that they like

mad [adjective]: an emotion that people feel when something happens that feels unfair

sad [adjective]: an emotion that people feel when something happens that is disappointing

scared [adjective]: an emotion that people feel when something happens that they can't control

sensation [noun]: information gathered by our body using the senses—taste, smell, touch, sight, hearing

Ping Pong Pressure
continued

Logan opens the door a crack and peeks in. Matias sits in the dark with his back against a storage shelf, hitting the ping-pong ball against the wall with his paddle.

"You okay?" Logan asks.

Matias nods. "You want to know why I play in the dark?"

Logan sits down next to her friend. "Sure."

"It's because whenever people see me play, they are excited about how good I am. But then I feel the pressure to *stay* good. And when I feel pressure about *staying* good, I don't feel what I usually feel when I play ping-pong."

"What do you usually feel when you play?" Logan asks, "You know, when people aren't pressuring you to CRUSH the competition?"

Matias is quiet for a moment before answering. "My mom gave me my first ping-pong ball and paddle to help me relax when I get frustrated. When I play, I don't feel pressure about school or life. It helps me just be in the moment. I feel like I'm in a calm bubble, and then I feel like I'm ready to face things that *are* making me stressed."

Logan winces. "And we came in and popped your calm bubble."

"Pretty much," Matias smiles, catching the ping-pong ball in his hand. "I think I'm ready to go back."

Logan and Matias leave the closet and start walking.

"New rule," Matias says confidently as he and Logan join their friends in the rec room. "If I'm playing ping-pong in the dark, the lights stay off. But once I'm done," he winks mischievously, "I'll play against you guys and CRUSH you all!"

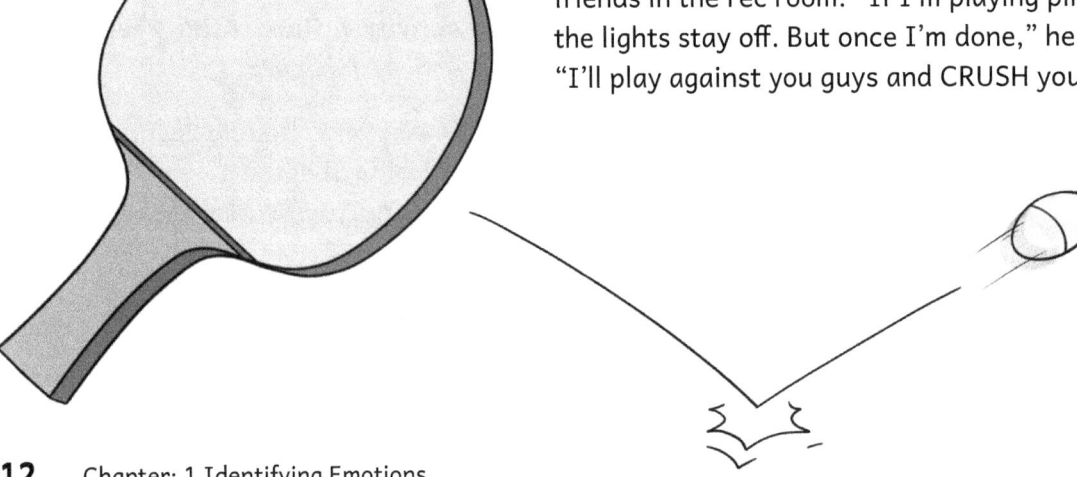

ACTIVITY OVERVIEW
Activity 1: The Mirror Game

OBJECTIVE
Students will practice observing and responding to the emotions of others using facial expressions in this fun and silly improv game.

MATERIALS
NA

PROMPT

A big part of how humans show their feelings is through facial expressions. Our brains have a particular way of understanding emotions by noticing how people move their faces and bodies. When I make this face, how do you think I am feeling? [Teachers can model 2-3 facial expressions, exaggerating each feeling.]

Today, we will practice identifying the feelings of others by playing The Mirror Game. The goal of the Mirror Game is to copy and guess others' feelings using what we notice in their facial expressions.

PROCEDURE

- Invite a student to the front of the group to be the "actor." The actor's role is to slowly move their face from one expression to another. For example, the actor can go from a happy smiling expression to an angry expression with a furrowed brow and sneering lips. The students will "mirror" the actor, matching the actor's expressions as they change. The more exaggerated and sillier the expressions, the more fun the game will be, and the easier for students to replicate the expressions.

- Let a few students take turns being the actor. The class will get comfortable with the activity as the actor runs through a series of emotions.

- After students have understood how the game works, ask the next actor to tell a story using only facial expressions and body language. Their expressions should include about three different emotions, showing the different parts of the story.

- When the actor is done, the group takes turns sharing the emotions they guessed the actor was showing with their expressions. Then, the actor can say what feelings they tried to convey.

CLOSURE

Closing discussion questions:

- Which expression was the most fun to act out? Which was the hardest to guess?
- Were there expressions that were similar to one another?
- What other strategies do you use to figure out what someone is feeling, other than their facial expressions?

Modification

Because reading people's facial expressions is difficult for some students, teachers can have those in the audience call out for a verbal clue. The actor can then give a verbal clue like, "Oh no!" if they are acting out being scared, or "Hooray!" if they are acting out being happy.

For adventurous groups, teachers can divide students into pairs to complete this activity versus inviting a single child to the front. Teachers should be careful in their partnerships to ensure that less outspoken students are paired with a student they are comfortable with.

ACTIVITY OVERVIEW
Activity 2: What Flavors Are Your Feelings?

OBJECTIVE
Students will use the Wheel of Feelings Flavors to deepen their understanding of emotions and become familiar with several words to help them better describe their feelings.

PROMPT

We all know the basic feelings: mad, sad, happy, surprised, and scared. There are many different flavors of each of these feelings. For example, you might be happy, but what kind of happy? Are you playful? Are you relaxed? Are you curious?

Today, we are going to turn our feelings into ice cream cones! An ice cream cone can have more than just one flavor. There are endless combinations, just like there are endless combinations of our feelings! You might have a triple scoop of happiness, topped with a nice sprinkle of relaxation. Or you might have a scoop of anger with a big dollop of frustration on top. That may not be an ice cream cone you want to eat often, but knowing how to name the flavor of the feelings can be helpful!

We will use the Wheel of Feelings Flavors handout as a tool to think more deeply about our feelings.

MATERIALS
- ✓ Flavorful Feelings Ice Cream Cone (downloadable PDF)
- ✓ Feelings Flavor Scenario Cards (downloadable PDF)
- ✓ Wheel of Feelings Flavors (downloadable PDF)
- ✓ Coloring materials

PROCEDURE
Name That Feeling Flavor Game:
- Cut out the scenario cards and choose one to model for the group. Read the scenario aloud and ask the students to use the Wheel of Feelings Flavors to identify which core feelings the character is feeling: happy, sad, mad, scared, or surprised.
- Next, have them add some flavor to that feeling by selecting from ice cream scoop choices in that category. For instance, if *happy* was the core feeling, their choices for flavors would be playful, joyful, peaceful, or engaged.

Make a Flavorful Feelings Cone:
- Hand out copies of the "Flavorful Feelings Ice Cream Cone" printable and give each student a scenario card. Ask students to read their cards and use the Wheel of Feelings Flavors to identify and write in the worksheet.
- Ask students to imagine how each of their character's feelings would taste and decorate their cone accordingly. Would a core feeling of happiness taste like strawberry ice cream? Would adding rainbow sprinkles add a dash of peace to the happiness? Let them get creative and use the flavors to explore how each emotion feels!

Modification
Ask students to pick a character from a favorite book and create a "Flavorful Feelings Ice Cream Cone" based on that character's feelings at a certain point in the book. They should pick one character on one page of the book to map their feelings. This is also a great way to connect to a read-aloud.

CLOSURE

Invite volunteers to share their ice cream cones. Prompt them to highlight their favorite part of their work with the group.

Display It! Have students cut out their ice cream cones. Hang up a copy of the Feelings Wheel at the center of the wall with the Flavorful Feelings Ice Cream Cone around it.

CHAPTER 1: Identifying Emotions | ACTIVITY 2: What Flavors Are Your Feelings?
Flavorful Feelings Ice Cream Cone

Name: _____ Date: _____

Core feeling is _____

Scoop feeling flavor is _____

This feeling flavor tastes like _____

Copyright © SuperDville   The Teacher's Toolbox For Every Child   **15**

CHAPTER 1: Identifying Emotions | ACTIVITY 2: What Flavors Are Your Feelings?

Feelings Flavor Scenario Cards

Cut the cards apart along the dotted lines.

- -

Scenario 1: Mel watched a scary movie yesterday. Afterward, he wanted to keep all the lights on, even when he went to sleep. When his mom poked her head into Mel's room to say goodnight, he screamed! What do you think Mel is feeling?

- -

Scenario 2: Jamie was working hard, building a spaceship out of blocks. His little brother, Devon, ran past and bumped the table, causing the spaceship to tip over and break in half. Jamie shouted, "Hey! You wrecked my ship," and chased after Devon. What do you think Jamie is feeling?

- -

Scenario 3: Vincent doesn't usually like science class, but today they are watching videos about volcanoes. Vincent can't take his eyes off the screen. He doesn't want the class to end! What do you think Vincent is feeling?

- -

Scenario 4: Ivan was excited to find a cookie on the counter when he returned from school. It was delicious! When his cousin got home an hour later, she started crying when she realized her cookie was gone. Ivan didn't know this cookie was special to her, and he didn't like to see his cousin upset. What do you think Ivan is feeling?

- -

Scenario 5: Judy is in line for the water fountain after gym class and is super thirsty. Jen is ahead of Judy and lets her friend, Alyssa, cut the line. Jen looks at Judy after Alyssa starts drinking and says, "You don't mind, right?" What do you think Judy is feeling?

- -

Scenario 6: Jack is hanging out with a group of kids he met at the park who all go to school together and have lots of inside jokes. Each time they start laughing about something Jack doesn't understand, he's unsure what to do. What do you think Jack is feeling?

- -

CHAPTER 1: Identifying Emotions | ACTIVITY 2: What Flavors Are Your Feelings?

Wheel of Feelings Flavors

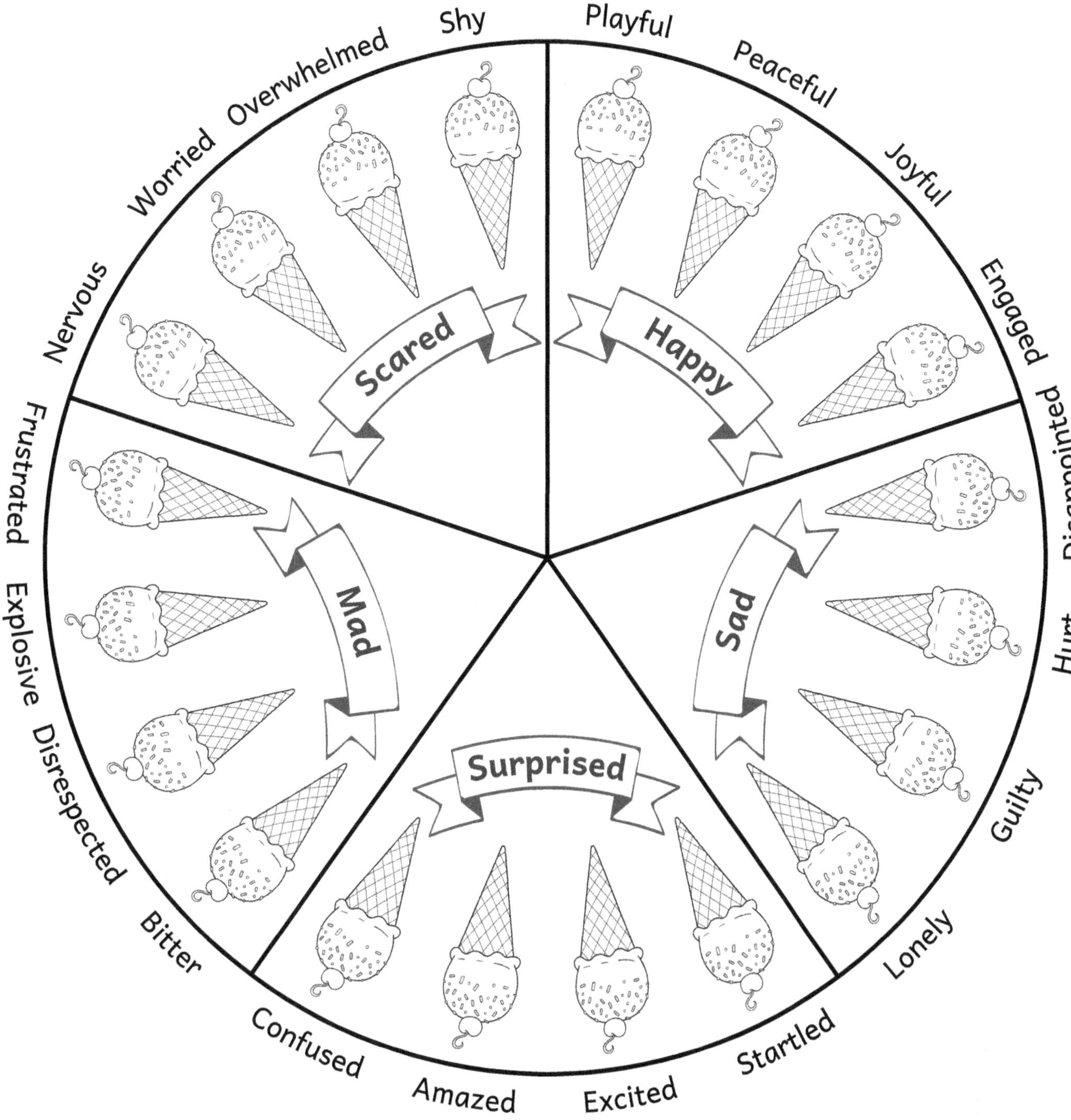

Shy, Playful, Peaceful, Joyful, Engaged, Disappointed, Hurt, Guilty, Lonely, Startled, Excited, Amazed, Confused, Bitter, Disrespected, Explosive, Frustrated, Nervous, Worried, Overwhelmed

Scared | Happy | Sad | Surprised | Mad

Copyright © SuperDville

The Teacher's Toolbox For Every Child **17**

ACTIVITY OVERVIEW
Activity 3: School Feelings

OBJECTIVE
Students will reflect on their feelings about different parts of the school day. This activity is primarily helpful for teachers to understand how students relate to academic challenges throughout their day. It is imperative that teachers create an environment where students feel safe to express their honest feelings.

MATERIALS
✓ Feelings Chart (downloadable PDF)

✓ Wheel of Feelings Flavors from Activity 2 (downloadable PDF)

PROMPT
During the school day, we all have favorite activities and activities that are less fun for us. As we go from class to class, we will have different feelings.

Today, you will use the Feelings Chart to share your feelings about different parts of the school day. I'm looking forward to learning which parts of the day are your favorites, and which you wish you could change. Knowing how you feel about each class helps me understand you and be a better teacher.

PROCEDURE
- Before class, complete the blank squares in the column on the left of the Feelings Chart. Some possible ways to complete the chart could include choosing to have students reflect on their academic subjects, compare easy and challenging parts of the day, or even to focus on particular classroom routines like circle time or transitions.

- Model how to fill out the worksheet with an example where you have mixed feelings. For instance, you might explain that an activity makes you both happy and a little scared. You would show that by coloring in four ice cream scoops in the "Happy" section and two in the "Scared" section.

- Have students complete the chart individually or in small groups.

Modification
Students can use the Wheel of Feelings Flavors to get specific about their emotions by selecting from the four flavors for each core feeling they have chosen.

CLOSURE
Closing discussion questions:
- What parts of the day give you good feelings? Why do you think that is?
- What parts of the day give you not-so-good feelings? Why do you think that is?
- What can help you feel the way you want to when you are at school?
- What can you do to improve the hard parts of the day?

CHAPTER 1: Identifying Emotions | ACTIVITY 3: School Feelings

Feelings Chart

Name: _____ Date: _____

	Happy	Sad	Mad	Scared	Surprised
	Happy	Sad	Mad	Scared	Surprised
	Happy	Sad	Mad	Scared	Surprised
	Happy	Sad	Mad	Scared	Surprised

ACTIVITY OVERVIEW
Activity 4: Illustrating Feelings

OBJECTIVE
Students will use this comparison activity to deepen their understanding of emotions. By drawing two different emotions, students will be challenged to think about each one with greater awareness, care, and curiosity.

PROMPT
We've discussed how important it is to understand our emotions. Sometimes, using creativity to learn more about our feelings can be helpful.

Today, we each will choose two emotions from our Wheel of Feelings Flavors handout and use art to show each other what it feels like inside our bodies when we experience the feelings we chose. Then, we will notice how the two feelings are different from one another.

MATERIALS
- ✓ Wheel of Feelings Flavors from Activity 2 (downloadable PDF)
- ✓ Paper
- ✓ Painting or coloring materials

PROCEDURE
- Students will choose two emotions from two different parts of the feelings wheel. For example, choosing peaceful and engaged would not be an ideal combination because they are both flavors of happiness. This will help ensure students have a clear comparison.
- Write the following instructions on the board:
  - Can you show how an emotion feels using colors, shapes, and textures?
- The goal is to get students to imagine the feeling, rather than situations when they would experience it or facial expressions that might represent it.
- Then, students will create a drawing or painting for each feeling. Allow them about 10 minutes to draw or paint.

Modification
For some students, showing examples of visual depictions of emotions created by artists may be helpful. This will be most effective if you choose two contrasting abstract works and engage students in a discussion comparing how each piece makes them feel. A pair could be "La Mancha Roja" by Joan Miro and "The Japanese Maple" by Helen Frankenthaler.

CLOSURE
Closing discussion questions:
- How did you choose to show your two emotions?
- What are the differences and similarities between your two drawings of the emotions?

ACTIVITY OVERVIEW
Extension Activities

EXTENSION 1:
Draw Your Own Flavorful Feelings Cone

Students can create their own Flavorful Feelings Cone to show their emotions about something from their own life. The cone is empty to enable students to include multiple flavors and a variety of toppings that show all of the different ingredients that make up their emotions.

Print Flavorful Feelings Ice Cream Cone from the downloadable PDF file.

EXTENSION 2:
What Does a Feeling Look Like Guessing Game

Teachers can hang up students' feelings art on the wall without any labels. Next, students do a gallery walk, write the feeling each picture gives them on a Post-it note, and leave it below each painting. Finally, the group can review their guesses and discuss the variety of emotional representations.

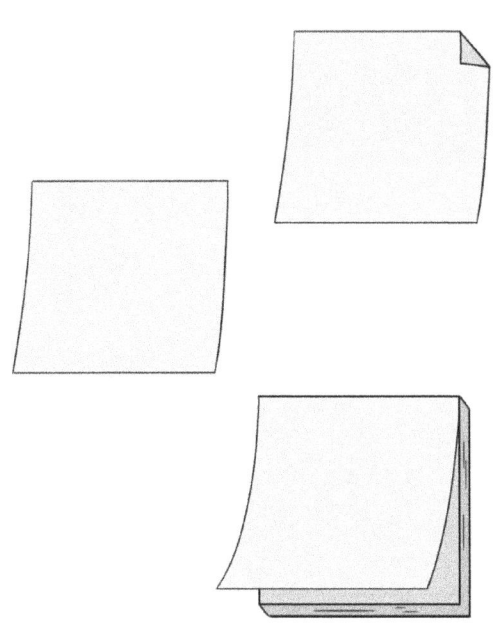

IDEAS & NOTES

_____
_____
_____
_____
_____
_____
_____
_____
_____

The Teacher's Toolbox For Every Child

 CHAPTER 1: Identifying Emotions | EXTENSION 1: Draw Your Own Flavorful Feelings Cone
Flavorful Feelings Ice Cream Cone

Name: _____ Date: _____

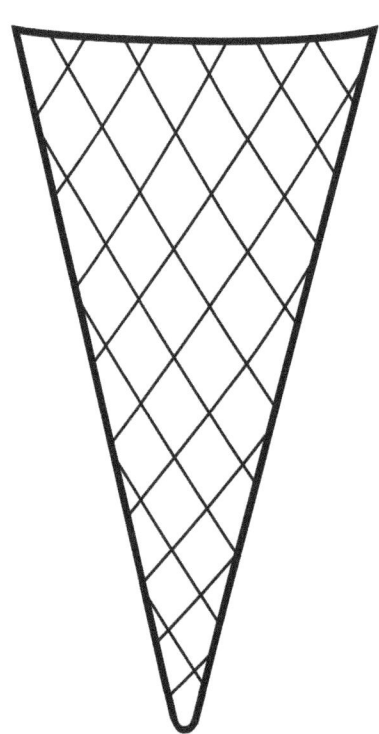

Core feeling is _____

Scoop feeling flavor is _____

This feeling flavor tastes like _____

Chapter 2:
Stress

Discussion Guide

READ ALOUD OBJECTIVE
Students will explore different stress management techniques and understand that everyone has different strategies that work best for them.

STORY SUMMARY
Kaia is stressed out about her homework. Her friends share strategies for dealing with stressful situations. Hudson shows yoga postures. Ari demonstrates his meditation practice. Ellie tells them she goes for a run when she feels stressed.

READ ALOUD INTRODUCTION
Everyone experiences stress—it's a normal, natural part of life. But just because it's natural to sometimes feel stressed, it doesn't mean we have to *stay* stressed. We can do many different things to relax our bodies and minds. We're going to read a story today about the different ways that a group of kids deal with stress. As you listen, think about which of their strategies you might have used in the past.

READ ALOUD CLOSURE
Finding ways to manage stress doesn't mean our problems will magically disappear, but it does mean that we will be better prepared to face those problems when we are calm.

LISTEN TO THE AUDIO VERSION OF THE STORY

COMPREHENSION QUESTIONS

1. **Why did Kaia get so stressed out?**
   Answer: Kaia got overwhelmed thinking about how much homework she had.

2. **What happened in Kaia's body when she got so stressed out?**
   Answer: Her chest felt tight, her hands were cold, and it was hard to breathe.

3. **What strategies did her friends share with Kaia to deal with her stress?**
   Answer: Hudson shared that he does yoga. Ari likes to meditate. Ellie exercises and listens to music.

DISCUSSION QUESTIONS

1. What are some things that make you feel stressed?

2. What tools do you know that help you relax when you are feeling stressed?

3. What tools have you tried that have not worked for you?

READ ALOUD:
Stress Mess

Kaia's teacher stands at the blackboard, scribbling line after line about the day's homework. The list goes on...and on...and on. Kaia frantically tries to write it all down in her planner, fighting to remember everything her teacher says.

"Read an article in the *New York Times* and summarize it thoroughly, finish your project for the upcoming science fair, read pages 1,000 to 2,000 in the textbook, take notes on questions 100 through 3,795...." Is Kaia hearing this right? Does she have thousands of pages of reading? It sure feels that way. And now her teacher is going on about physics, making a radio using bubble gum, studying rocket science, and...

Later, as Kaia sits on a bench in the playground, she can't stop thinking about her homework while her friends play. She feels her chest tighten as she remembers the long list of things she has to do. Her hands feel cold, and it's suddenly harder to breathe. Everything starts to get blurry, until...

"Are you okay, Kaia?" Ari asks. As Kaia's vision clears, she sees Ari and Hudson leaning in close, looking concerned.

Kaia says, "I was just thinking about how much homework I have, and I got so anxious and nervous and scared..."

"You have a lot of homework, huh?" Hudson sighs. "That's tough."

"I know how that feels," Ari agrees.

"All this pressure started building in my chest," Kaia explains. "And it was a little hard to breathe."

"You'll be alright," Ari says reassuringly. "We're here with you, and it will be OK."

"I guess," Kaia sighs. "But why do I get so anxious, though? I try to ignore it until it goes away, but it always comes back!" Kaia starts to look a little queasy.

"Ignoring stress is *not* the best way to make it go away," Ari tells Kaia.

"I might have a different strategy for you," Hudson says. "I do yoga to help me relax."

Kaia is surprised. "You do yoga?" She can't believe what Hudson is saying.

Hudson nods with a grin. "Yoga helps me calm my mind. When I just focus on one thing at a time, like my breath, I feel so much better! And it feels really good to stretch and hold a

continued next page

Chapter 2 Activities

Activity 1: **Stressed Body / Calm Body**
Activity Type: Discussion

Activity 2: **De-stressing Strategies**
Activity Type: Worksheet

Activity 3: **Best Fit Strategy**
Activity Type: Discussion

Activity 4: **What Can I Control?**
Activity Type: Worksheet

Extension 1: **Stressed Body / Calm Body Printable**
Activity Type: Worksheet

Extension 2: **De-stressing Dance Party**
Activity Type: Movement

SEL Vocabulary

anxiety [noun]: when the body stays in a state of stress over a long period and can't get calm even when there is no danger present

cope [verb]: to find ways to feel calm when stressors are making it hard to do

coping strategy [noun]: a tool or strategy that reminds the body that it isn't in danger and helps reduce stress

meditation [noun]: a way of calming the body and mind using breathing, visualization, or purposeful attention

stress [noun]: a set of ways the body gets ready to handle something difficult or scary, including changes in our breathing, heartbeat, and even digestion

stressor [noun]: an event, challenge, or situation that causes stress

sensation [noun]: information about the body or the world around captured by one of the senses: sight, hearing, touch, taste, smell

yoga [noun]: a cultural practice originated in ancient India that uses movement, breathing, and meditation to calm the mind

Stress Mess

continued

pose." Hudson stands up and leads his friends over to the grass. "Let me show you."

Together, the kids stretch to do a tree pose. Ari gets a little stuck and falls on the grass.

"Yoga isn't my thing," Ari says from the ground. "But since I'm down here already, let me show you what I do when I'm stressed. I meditate!"."

All the kids gather to sit on the grass and cross their legs like Ari.

"In through your nose and out through your mouth," Ari says in a calm voice. "Count to four on every breath in and out

Quietly, the friends breathe together, getting more and more relaxed. But then, Ellie comes running up to the group. "What are you guys doing?" Ellie yells with a grin, startling her friends out of their peaceful calm.

"We're finding ways to relieve our stress," Ari explains.

"We did yoga, and now we're practicing meditation and breathing," Hudson adds.

"Cool," Ellie says. "Have you guys tried exercising? I like to run and listen to music. It calms me down and clears my head."

Kaia smiles as Ellie gets the group up and moving along with her favorite exercise routine. Hudson, Ari, and Ellie cheer, happy to have helped their friend.

ACTIVITY OVERVIEW
Activity 1: Stressed Body / Calm Body

OBJECTIVE
Students will compare and contrast the way they feel when they are stressed and when they are calm. They will use this knowledge to help them identify how stress feels in their bodies.

MATERIALS
- ✓ Two sheets of poster paper, one labeled "Stressed" and one labeled "Calm"
- ✓ Markers

PROMPT

Sometimes, we don't notice that stress is building up inside of us until we're overwhelmed. One way to avoid becoming overwhelmed with stress is by taking time to notice the sensations in our bodies when we are stressed and when we are calm. That way, we'll recognize how these sensations in our bodies and minds shift when stress begins to build.

Today, we will use our imaginations to help name the sensations we feel when we're calm and when we are stressed.

PROCEDURE
- Prompt students to imagine two scenarios. For example:
  - A stressful situation, like when they have a test and don't feel prepared.
  - A relaxing situation, like when they have finished all their homework and will meet up with friends.
- First, ask students to silently imagine a stressful situation. Ask them to notice what they feel in their bodies as they imagine. Lead them through their sensory exploration using the questions below. Record their responses on the "Stressed" poster paper. Be sure to validate that each body can have different sensations for the same feeling.
  - What do you notice about the way you are breathing?
  - What can you feel in your chest and throat?
  - What can you feel in your belly, arms, and legs?
  - What else do you notice?
- Next, encourage students to take in and let out a deep, calming breath to reset from the stressful situation they just imagined. Now, ask students to recall a time when they felt calm and at ease. Follow the same process above and record their answers on the "Calm" poster paper.

Modification
Allow students to write down their observations on Post-its and add them anonymously to the poster paper. This may be helpful for groups who are shy about sharing their feelings.

Allow students to write their responses directly on the poster. This is useful for groups who need opportunities to move.

CLOSURE
Compare the two posters as a group. Closing discussion questions:
- What do you notice about the sensations on the calm body side? How about in the stressed body side?
- Are there any sensations that come up on both sides?
- Are there any sensations that surprised you?

ACTIVITY OVERVIEW
Activity 2: De-stressing Strategies

OBJECTIVE
Students will create an inventory with strategies they prefer to use to deal with stressors. They will learn about the two types of strategy: Breaks and Problem Solvers. They will also understand the need to utilize both to address their stressors better.

MATERIALS
- ✓ Strategy Bank (downloadable PDF)
- ✓ Strategy List (downloadable PDF)
- ✓ Scissors
- ✓ Glue Sticks
- ✓ Writing materials
- ✓ Optional - laminating machine

PROMPT
When we are feeling stressed or anxious, it can be hard to remember all the different strategies we can choose from to help us feel better.

We could use a *Take a Break* strategy, like going for a walk or dancing to your favorite song. Or we could use a *Problem Solver* strategy, like making a plan to tackle what's challenging us or talking to someone we trust.

Today, each of us will use a "Strategy Bank" worksheet as an easy way for our class to "save up" all the different strategies we can use when feeling stressed or anxious.

PROCEDURE
- Teachers can have students cut out squares from the Strategy List printable and paste them into their Strategy Bank worksheet. Students must choose four strategies they like to *Take a Break* and four *Problem Solver* strategies that help them deal with their stressors.
- They can use the pre-written strategies or write or draw their own. Inventories can be laminated and used as support when students become upset or overwhelmed.

CLOSURE
Choose a place for students to keep their strategy banks and let them know that they can use these tools when they feel overwhelmed.

Closing discussion questions:
- Which strategies have you already used?
- Which ones are you most excited to try out?

CHAPTER 2: Stress | ACTIVITY 2: De-stressing Strategies

Strategy Bank

Name: _____ Date: _____

Problem Solvers	

Take a Break	

CHAPTER 2: Stress | ACTIVITY 2: De-stressing Strategies

Strategy List

Take a walk	Talk to someone you trust	Break it into smaller steps
Draw	Exercise	Take slow breaths
Dance	Go outside	Drink water
Journal	Make a plan	Listen to music
Stretch	Grab a snack	Ask for help
Laugh	Use a fidget	Play a game

ACTIVITY OVERVIEW
Activity 3: Best Fit Strategy

OBJECTIVE
Students will compare different coping strategies for dealing with stress. They will consider how different scenarios call for different strategies. Some situations make *Taking a Break* a good choice, and some call for a *Problem Solver* strategy.

This activity works best if students have already completed Activity 2: De-stressing Strategy Bank. They should understand the two strategy types, Breaks and Problem Solvers.

MATERIALS
- ✓ Best-Fit Strategy Scenario Cards (downloadable PDF)
- ✓ Optional: Strategy Bank from Activity 2 (downloadable PDF)

PROMPT

We've been experimenting over the last few classes with different strategies for dealing with stress. Not every strategy fits every situation.

The best-fit strategy helps us become more able to deal with the things that stress us. For instance, playing video games can sometimes be helpful to calm down. However, they can also distract us from what we need to do, leaving us more stressed out than before, especially if we play for an extended period.

Today, we will look at different situations and decide the best-fit strategies for dealing with each.

PROCEDURE
- Write the definition of a best-fit strategy on the board: "The best-fit strategy will be the most effective solution for a particular stressful situation."
- Break students into groups of two or three. Have each group review one scenario card. Have the kids decide whether the child in the scenario has picked a best-fit strategy for their situation.
- If they decide the child hasn't found the best-fit strategy, students should use the Strategy Bank to choose what they think is the best-fit strategy and explain why.
- If they think the child in the scenario has already found a good strategy, students should use the Strategy Bank to find other strategies that might work as well.

CLOSURE
Closing discussion questions:
- Which *Problem Solver strategy* is the best-fit solution?
- What are some situations where a *Take a Break strategy* is the best-fit strategy?
- What makes a strategy the right one at that moment?

The Teacher's Toolbox For Every Child

CHAPTER 2: Stress | ACTIVITY 3: Best Fit Strategy

Best-Fit Strategy Scenario Cards

Cut the cards apart along the dotted lines.

 —

Scenario 1: Penny has a test tomorrow and has an hour before dinner to study. She sits down to study for the test but is so overwhelmed that her stomach starts hurting, and her mind spins with worry. Penny keeps imagining failing the test and getting a big, red F.

Penny sets aside her homework, and plays a game on her tablet. She forgets all about studying for the test, which makes her feel a bit better until she realizes it's time for dinner and she hasn't studied at all. Now Penny feels worse than she did before!

- What was Penny's strategy for dealing with her stress about the test?
- Was this the best-fit strategy? Why or why not?
- What are some options for a best-fit strategy that you would recommend?

— —

Scenario 2: Tim was playing basketball with Ben during morning recess. He was running toward the hoop for a jump shot when he tripped and fell, sending the basketball flying.

Ben laughed hard as he caught the ball and watched as Tim scrambled up. Tim's cheeks got red hot, and his knees stung. "Where are you going?" Ben called, still laughing, as Tim hurried off the court. "You can take another shot!"

Tim kept imagining Ben's laughing face for the rest of the day and felt his cheeks get hot again. After school, Tim saw Ben, and before Ben could laugh at him again, Tim said, "What's up, loser?"

- What was Tim's strategy for dealing with his stress about feeling embarrassed in front of his friend?
- Was this the best-fit strategy?
- What are some options for a best-fit strategy you would recommend?

— —

ACTIVITY OVERVIEW
Activity 4: What I Can and Can't Control

OBJECTIVE
Students will explore how to identify what they can and cannot control when in a stressful situation.

MATERIALS
✓ What I Can and Can't Control (downloadable PDF)
✓ Whiteboard or poster paper

PROMPT
When we're in a stressful situation, it can feel like there is nothing we can do to make it better. Imagine it rains on the day we plan to play at the park. It might feel like the whole day is ruined. But if we pause, and consider that while we can't stop the rain, we can still have fun.

Today, we will use the What I Can and Can't Control printable to learn how to identify what is in our control and what isn't when we're in a stressful situation. Learning this strategy will help us deal with challenging situations.

PROCEDURE
- Make a T-chart on the board with the categories "I Can Control" and "I Can't Control."
- Lead the group by brainstorming events and actions in and out of their control.
- Take notes on the board of suggestions. Guide the students to notice that what is in their control are their actions and their words.
- Next, let students independently complete the What I Can and Can't Control printable. They can use examples from the class brainstorm or come up with some new ones of their own.

CLOSURE
Invite volunteers to share with the group. Prompt them to highlight one example of something they can't control and one example of something they can control from their worksheet.

The Teacher's Toolbox For Every Child

CHAPTER 2: Stress | ACTIVITY 4: What I Can and Can't Control

What I Can and Can't Control

Name: _____   Date: _____

I can't control

I can control

My Words

My Actions

_____
_____
_____
_____

ACTIVITY OVERVIEW
Extension Activities

EXTENSION 1:
Stressed Body / Calm Body

Older students can create their own Stressed Body / Calm Body chart to help them notice the sensations that show up when they are feeling stressed and when they are feeling calm.

Print Stress Body / Calm Body printable from the downloadable PDF file.

Teachers can use this printable to check in with students about their feelings.

EXTENSION 2:
De-stressing Dance Party

Students can create a playlist of five to ten songs that make them feel happy, relaxed, and confident.

The playlist can be a written list of song titles, or students can use technology like Spotify or YouTube to create a playlist that teachers can pull from for dance parties and movement breaks in the classroom.

IDEAS & NOTES

_____
_____
_____
_____
_____
_____
_____
_____

CHAPTER 2: Stress | EXTENSION 1: Stressed Body / Calm Body

Stressed Body / Calm Body

Name: _____ Date: _____

Stressed Body   **Calm Body**

36   Chapter: 2 Stress   Copyright © SuperDville

Chapter 3:
Perseverance

Discussion Guide

READ ALOUD OBJECTIVE
Students will learn about perseverance and why it is a necessary trait to help them overcome challenges.

STORY SUMMARY
Jace is down on himself for getting a low score on a spelling test and feels like he should just give up trying to improve his spelling. But his friends encourage him to keep trying. Jordan shares a story about the best advice a teacher ever gave her: "The only things you can fail at are the things you give up on." Jace takes this story to heart and decides he won't give up. He learns he can get better at spelling with perseverance!

READ ALOUD INTRODUCTION
Can you think of a time when you tried something that was so hard that you felt like giving up? Today, we will read a story about a kid named Jace facing a frustrating challenge that makes him want to give up. Let's see how he decides to deal with his problem. As you listen, think about what you might do if you were in his shoes.

READ ALOUD CLOSURE
Perseverance means not giving up, even when things are hard. The best thing about perseverance is that it's a trait we all have—even if we've never used it! This means the next time we want to give up because something is hard, we can remember that we know how to persevere, and if we keep trying, we can overcome our challenges.

LISTEN TO THE AUDIO VERSION OF THE STORY

COMPREHENSION QUESTIONS

1. Why was Jace unhappy?
   Answer: He did not think he scored well on his spelling quiz.

2. How did Jace want to deal with his problem?
   Answer: He wanted to give up.

3. Why was Jordan proud of herself for her quiz score even though it wasn't as high as her peers?
   Answer: It was better than she'd done all year.

DISCUSSION QUESTIONS

1. How do you think Jace felt when he studied hard and got a six on his next spelling test?

2. What do you think it meant when Mr. Scott said, "The only things you can fail at are the things you give up on?"

3. Perseverance is the skill of not giving up even when you feel like something you want is impossible. When Jace keeps practicing spelling, even though it is hard for him, he shows perseverance.

   Can you think of a time when you showed perseverance?

READ ALOUD:
Never Give Up

Ellie and Jordan are hanging out in the rec room after school, shooting toy basketballs through the hoop above the door.

Jordan shoots a ball and scores.

"Nice!" says Ellie.

"Slam dunk!" claps Jordan.

Jace stomps into the rec room with a big frown. He crumbles up a piece of paper and slams it through the hoop so hard that the hoop pops off and falls to the floor. Jace doesn't stop to pick it up. He just throws himself on the couch, his arms crossed in front of him.

Ellie and Jordan exchange a look. "What did that basketball hoop ever do to you?" Jordan jokes, "You slam-dunked it right off the door."

"Sorry," Jace grumbles. "I'm not mad at the hoop. I'm mad at what I put through it."

Ellie picks up the crumpled paper and checks what's on it. "You got a 6 out of 10 on your spelling test. You could have done worse!" she reassures him.

Chapter 3 Activities

Activity 1: **Perseverance Comic**
Activity Type: Art

Activity 2: **Perseverance Role Play**
Activity Type: Role Play

Activity 3: **Goal Setting**
Activity Type: Craft

Activity 4: **An Inspiring Thought**
Activity Type: Worksheet

Extension 1: **What Happens Next?**
Activity Type: Art

Extension 2: **Working Toward My Goal**
Activity Type: Worksheet

"Yeah, but all the other kids got 8s, 9s, and 10s and didn't even study!" Jace says unhappily.

Ellie says, "Wait, didn't you get a 4 out of 10 on your last spelling test? That means you're getting better!"

"So what?" Jace huffs in frustration. "I'll never be good at spelling, so why even try? I give up!"

Ellie's encouragement is not working, so Jordan tries something else.

"Hold on there, Jace. Let me tell you a story."

Jace crosses his arms tighter and sighs, but he listens to Jordan.

"It was the day before summer vacation last year," Jordan begins, "and Mr. Scott had just handed back our final math tests. Do you know what I got? A 6 out of 10."

"Just like me!" Jace says, sitting up. "You got really mad, right?"

"Nope," Jordan says. "Because it was the highest grade I got all year. Six out of ten was my best score yet!"

"Same," Jace says, his brow furrowed. "I didn't think of it like that."

Jordan nods. "That's why when Mr. Scott asked us to raise a hand if we were proud of our scores, I shot my hand straight up."

continued next page

SEL Vocabulary

compare [verb]: to notice how two things are the same and/or different

encouragement [noun]: words or actions that make someone more determined, hopeful, or confident

fixed mindset [noun]: believing that knowledge and skills are like a light switch, either one has that skill or they don't

frustration [noun]: the upset feeling when one can't change or do something when they want to

frustration tolerance [noun]: the amount of frustration one can handle without giving up

goal [noun]: an end result that someone works toward

growth mindset [noun]: believing it is possible to learn and develop skills through practice

improve [verb]: to become better at something

perseverance [noun]: the skill of not giving up when you feel like something you want is impossible

persistent [adjective]: when one keeps trying to do things even though it is hard or they had failed previously

Never Give Up
continued

Jace now listens closely.

"But then," Jordan continues, "Tim peeked at my paper and yelled out, 'She only got a 6 out of 10!' and the rest of the kids all laughed."

"That's awful!" Ellie and Jace say together.

"It was," Jordan agrees. "Luckily, my teacher, Mr. Scott, spoke up. He said I had every right to be proud because I'd worked hard in math all year and had improved my grades."

Jace grinned, "Mr. Scott sounds pretty awesome."

"That's not even the best part!" Jordan said, "Mr. Scott gave me the most helpful tip. He said, *'The only things you can fail at are the things you give up on.'*"

"The only things you can fail at..." Ellie repeats.

"...are the things you give up on." Jace finishes with a smile.

"Right!" Jordan continues. "So I kept working on my math. I even did flashcards over the summer."

"I remember that!" Jace says, "You even worked on them while we waited for the camp bus."

"Yep. And on the first test of the year, I got two points more than I'd ever gotten before!" Jordan says proudly.

"That's pretty impressive."

"It's my never-give-up work ethic," Jordan says with a grin. "I'm telling you: keep working on your spelling, and you will get better. That's called perseverance!"

"And remember," Ellie chimes in. "Don't worry about what other kids are doing. Just focus on yourself!"

After that, Jace makes sure to study his spelling every day. On his next spelling test, Jace cheers when he gets a six out of ten. And he cheers even louder when he gets a 7 out of 10 on the next test!

He promises himself never to give up ever again.

ACTIVITY OVERVIEW
Activity 1: Perseverance Comic

OBJECTIVE
Students will reflect on a time when they faced a challenge and how their response impacted the situation's outcome.

MATERIALS
- ✓ Perseverance Comic Strip (downloadable PDF)
- ✓ Crayons, pencils, colored pencils, or markers

PROMPT

In the story "Never Give Up," Jordan encourages her friend Jace by sharing a story about when she worked hard and got her best score ever in math. She explains how even though her score was lower than her classmates, she still felt proud of her progress. She says, "I'm telling you: keep working on your spelling, and you will get better!"

Today, we will create our own comic strips all about perseverance. Think about a time when something was hard for you, and you thought about giving up, but you did not.

How did you feel when you wanted to give up? What did you do instead of giving up? Draw a picture or write sentences/a paragraph to describe this experience.

PROCEDURE

- Have the class brainstorm as a group about things that were hard the first time they tried. Some examples include riding a bike, doing long division, or drawing realistic animals. Record student answers on the board.
- Once the group has a list of ideas, have students begin to draw in their blank comic strips. The first square should show what the challenge was, the second should show how they responded, and the third should show the result of their actions.

Modification

If preferred, students who like to draw can create their own comic layout.

Students who like writing more than drawing can choose to create a written story or a poem rather than a comic.

CLOSURE

- Invite volunteers to share their comics.
- Prompt them to highlight their favorite part of their work with the group.

CHAPTER 3: Perseverance | ACTIVITY 1: Perseverance Comic

Perseverance Comic Strip

Name: _____ Date: _____

ACTIVITY OVERVIEW
Activity 2: Perseverance Role Play

OBJECTIVE
Students will demonstrate an understanding of perseverance by acting out scenarios.

MATERIALS
✓ Perseverance Scenario Cards (downloadable PDF)

PROMPT
We have learned about perseverance and the importance of remembering that when we struggle or fail, it is a sign that we are growing and improving. Sometimes, giving up seems like an easy choice, especially when it is hard to imagine what it looks or feels like to keep going.

Today, we will work in groups to act out different scenarios. Each group will get a chance to imagine what would happen if their character gives up, and what might happen if they persevere and keep trying.

PROCEDURE
- Put students in pairs and pass out a scenario to each group.
- Each scenario has a main character trying to persevere. A second character is with them, either discouraging them or supporting them.
- The pairs act out the same scenario twice. In the first version of the scene, students portray the main character giving up. In the second version, students show their character finding a way to persevere.
- Encourage the students to act out the emotions of each character as well.
- Give the groups 5 minutes to practice each outcome.
- Bring the class back together and allow each group to perform their scenes in front of the group.

CLOSURE
Closing discussion questions:
- How did the characters seem after they gave up? Were they happy, sad, ashamed, worried... or something else?
- What did you notice the characters did when they kept going?
Was it easy or hard? What is it like to struggle and then persevere?
- What did the main characters' friends, teachers and parents do to support them? Can you think of other ways to encourage your friends when they struggle?

The Teacher's Toolbox For Every Child

CHAPTER 3: Perseverance | ACTIVITY 2: Perseverance Role Play

Perseverance Scenario Cards

Cut the cards apart along the dotted lines.

Scenario 1   **Roles:** Dante, Max

Dante wants to try out for the travel baseball team, but Max tells him he'll never make it because he misses the ball so often.

Scenario 2   **Roles:** Ava, Ava's piano teacher

Ava wants to learn how to play her favorite pop song on the piano, but there are symbols on the sheet music that she has never seen before. Her piano teacher suggests that they start by learning the first symbol on the page.

Scenario 3   **Roles:** Lucas, Ray

Lucas is the only gymnast in his class who hasn't mastered his round-off. Ray has moved on to back handsprings, and Lucas feels like he is left behind.

Scenario 4   **Roles:** Priya, Priya's mom

Priya hates math class. She thinks it's boring and hard. If she doesn't finish her math homework this week, her mom has told her she can't try out for the school play.

ACTIVITY OVERVIEW
Activity 3: Goal Setting

OBJECTIVE
Students will write goals for themselves. They will create a clear picture of the desired outcome they can display in the classroom for motivation.

MATERIALS
- ✓ Goal Flag Template (downloadable PDF)
- ✓ Coloring materials
- ✓ Scissors

PROMPT
Often, we forget that we had to learn to do things that might seem easy to us today, like walking and talking. Did you know it takes babies about a year to start walking? Then, at least another six months before they can run and jump.

When we decide to learn something new, we need to practice and work at it over time. Sometimes, that can be boring or frustrating, so it helps to remind ourselves of our goals and how far we've come.

Today, we will create a Goal Flag for something we hope to accomplish. The flag will help us visualize our goals using pictures and words. After we are done, we will hang the flags up in the classroom as a reminder of what we are working for when we struggle or are impatient with our progress.

PROCEDURE
- Students choose one goal they want to achieve by the end of the school year. Go through the planning questions on page two of the printable as a class. Teachers can assist students by scribing their answers to the first two questions. Kids can write or draw the steps they'll need to follow to achieve their goals.
- After the class completes the planning section, students can cut out their flags and illustrate the front. Prompt students to use words and designs to show, with as much detail as possible, what it will be like when they achieve their goal. Prompt them to deepen their thinking with questions like:
  - What emotions will you feel when you achieve your goal?
  - Who will be with you?
  - What will it sound/smell/feel/look like?
  - How will you celebrate?

CLOSURE
Hang the flags so that students can see them all together.

Closing discussion questions:
- What do you notice about all the flags hanging together?
- What illustrations do you like from your classmate's work? Why?
- What are some ways that you could support your classmates in achieving their goals?

The Teacher's Toolbox For Every Child

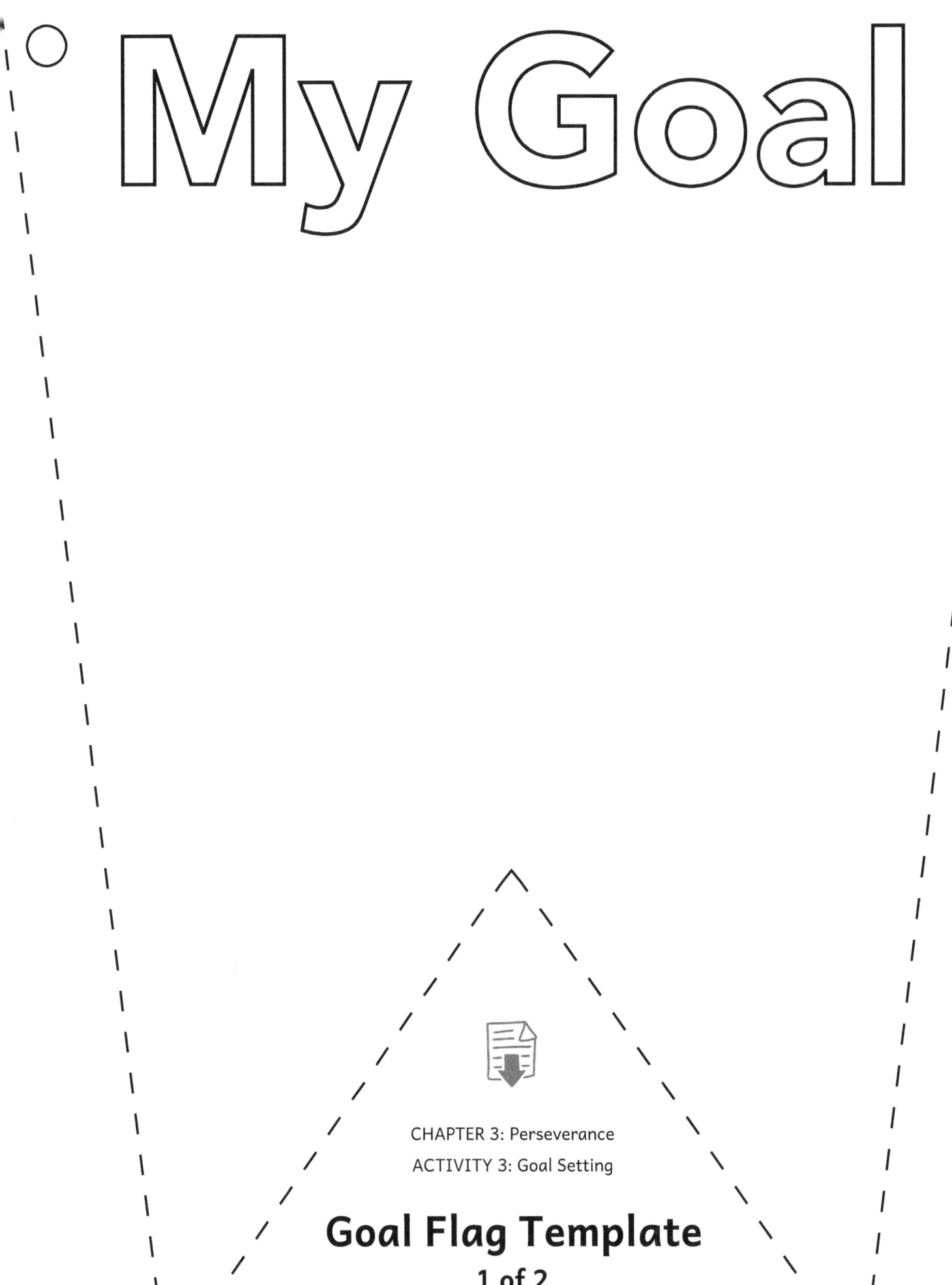

CHAPTER 3: Perseverance
ACTIVITY 3: Goal Setting

**Goal Flag Template
1 of 2**

My goal is to:

____

____

This goal is important to me because:

____

____

The things I will need to do to achieve the goal are:

____

____

CHAPTER 3: Perseverance

ACTIVITY 3: Goal Setting

Goal Flag Template

2 of 2

ACTIVITY OVERVIEW

Activity 4: An Inspiring Thought

OBJECTIVE
Students will create a piece of art with a message that is personally motivating for them.

MATERIALS
- ✓ Inspiring Quotes (downloadable PDF)
- ✓ Coloring materials
- ✓ Optional: Other decorative items such as stickers, glitter, etc.
- ✓ Optional: Printed quote and glue

PROMPT
In the story "Never Give Up," Jace is upset about getting a low test score. He wants to give up, but his friends remind him he can improve with practice. Jordan reminds him of the tip her teacher gave her, "The only things you can fail at are the things you give up on."

Today, we will think about this quote and its meaning. Then, we will make inspirational cards or posters with our own motivational phrases to display on a refrigerator at home or bulletin boards and walls in class.

Can you think of other motivational or inspirational words that remind you not to give up?

PROCEDURE
- Read and display the quote, "The only things you can fail at are the things you give up on," for students to see.
- Ask students how they feel when they hear those words.
- Have the class look at the motivational quotes printable. Ask students to think about what they would say to someone struggling to persevere, and write it in the space provided on the printable.
- Allow students to create a piece of art incorporating their own words or one of the sayings from the printable.

CLOSURE
Closing discussion questions:
- Why did you choose this quote?
- What does it mean to you?
- Where will you post your card or poster so you'll be inspired to persevere when things get challenging?

CHAPTER 3: Perseverance | ACTIVITY 4: An Inspiring Thought

Inspiring Quotes

Name: _____ Date: _____

"Fall seven times and stand up eight."
-Japanese Proverb

"Every strike brings me closer to the next home run."
-Babe Ruth

"You can't be afraid to make mistakes. They're not the end of the world."
-Simone Biles

"It always seems impossible until it is done."
-Nelson Mandela

My inspiring thought:

" _____
_____
_____
_____ "

ACTIVITY OVERVIEW
Extension Activities

EXTENSION 1:
What Happens Next?

Students can add to their perseverance comic by exploring what would happen next in the story. What might their next move be based on the result of their actions in the initial activity?

Print What Happens Next? from the downloadable PDF file.

EXTENSION 2:
Working Toward My Goal

Students can fill in one box on the Goal Tracking Sheet each time they work on their goal.

Print Working Toward My Goal from the downloadable PDF file.

Teachers can offer encouragement, focusing on how much effort students have put into practice. The purpose of the goal tracker is not to provide rewards or reinforcements but to help the students visualize and develop pride in their efforts.

IDEAS & NOTES

_____
_____
_____
_____
_____
_____
_____
_____

CHAPTER 3: Perseverance | EXTENSION 1: What Happens Next?

What Happens Next?

Name: _____ Date: _____

BEFORE

DAY 1

DAY 2

DAY 3

AFTER

Copyright © SuperDville

CHAPTER 3: Perseverance | EXTENSION ACTIVITY 2: Working Toward My Goal

Working Toward My Goal

Name: _____   Date: _____

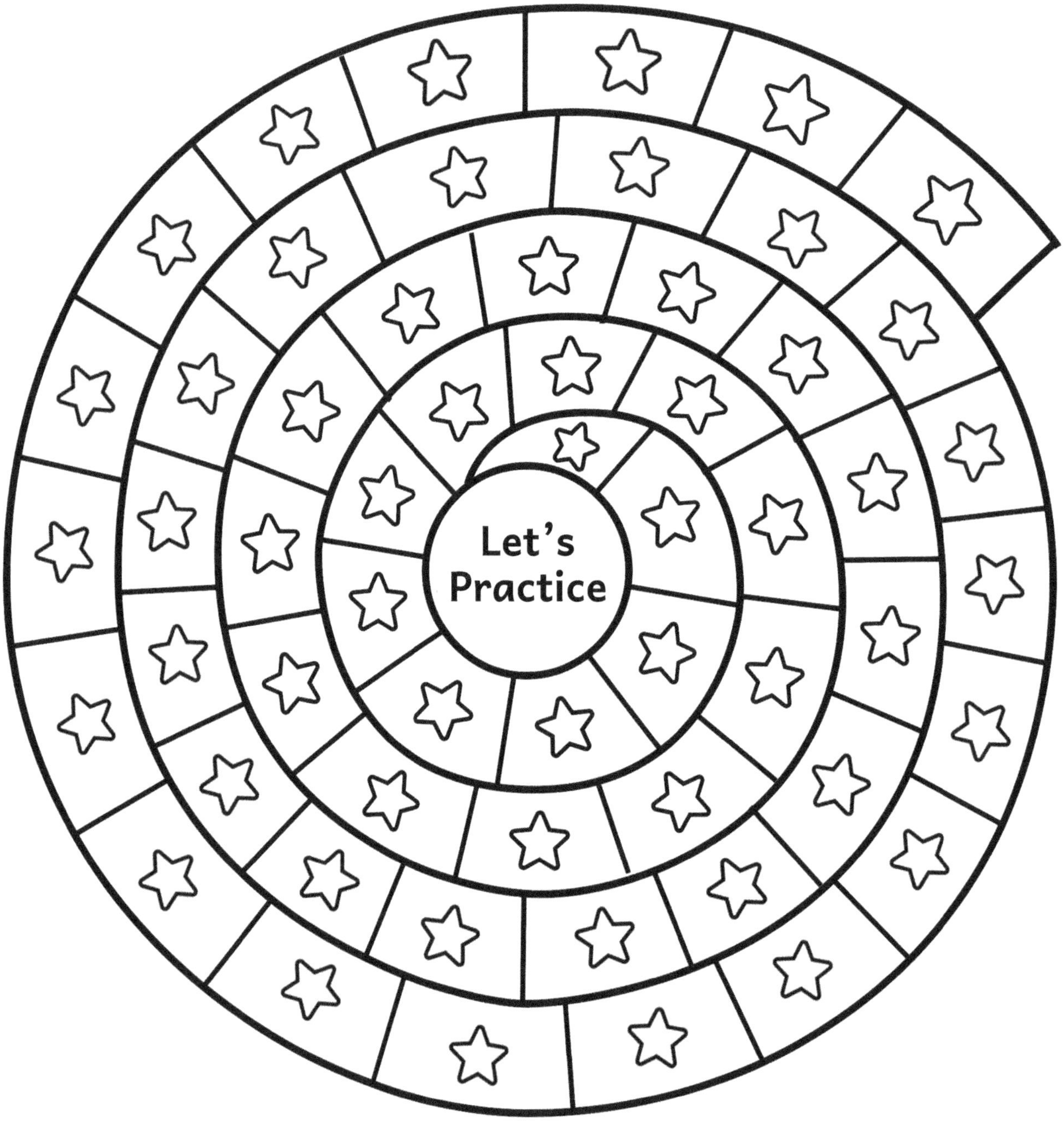

(Spiral of star-filled spaces leading to center labeled "Let's Practice")

My Goal: _____

Chapter 4:
Gratitude

Discussion Guide

READ ALOUD OBJECTIVE
Students will learn how finding reasons to be grateful can make a bad day better.

> **STORY SUMMARY**
> Ari gets lost on his way to the ball field. A wizard helps him find his way. Although the day doesn't go as planned, Ari still feels grateful in the end!

READ ALOUD INTRODUCTION
When we're having a bad day, it's easy to just focus on everything that's gone wrong. *I woke up late, missed the bus, and forgot my lunch!*

But what would happen if we also listed the good things about our day? What if we paused a moment, took a deep breath, and found things we were grateful for? *A friend saved me a seat. We watched a cool video in science. I scored a goal in gym class.*

Scientists have discovered that focusing on what we are grateful for is healthy for our brains! Gratitude can keep our bodies and minds healthy; it also feels good! As we read our story today, think about what the main character can be grateful for—even as he faces challenges.

READ ALOUD CLOSURE
When it feels like everything is going wrong, taking a moment to remember the things we're grateful for can help us feel better. This can help change our perspective from thinking that everything is awful to recognizing that there are wonderful things that we can be grateful for.

LISTEN TO THE AUDIO VERSION OF THE STORY

COMPREHENSION QUESTIONS

1. **Why did Ari arrive late to the ball field?**
   Answer: Ari got lost on the way to the ball field.

2. **What strategies did the wizard show Ari to tell his left from right?**
   Answer: He showed Ari how to use a Visual Representation using colored stars such as ruby red for right and lime green for left.

3. **What happened after Ari left the wizard?**
   Answer: He found his way to the ball field using the helpful strategies the wizard shared to tell his left from his right.

DISCUSSION QUESTIONS

1. What emotions might Ari have felt when he sat under the tree thinking he missed the game?

2. Can you think of a time when someone helped you with something important, like the wizard helping Ari?

3. Using creative solutions, the wizard showed Ari a different way to tell his right from left. Have you ever had to find a creative way to help yourself or someone else when something was hard for you?

54 Chapter: 4 Gratitude

READ ALOUD:
Lost In The Park

Today is the school's annual softball game and Ari is very late. Racing into the park, he stops at a hot dog vendor. Panting, Ari asks, "Do you know where the ball field is?"

"Sure do," the vendor nods. He takes out a napkin and draws a map. As he draws, he lists a long series of directions for Ari.

Ari grabs the napkin and thanks the man as he runs down a path.

Ari runs deeper and deeper into the park. He takes a right, then another right, and left and...he slows down and finally stops.

"Oh no," he pants miserably, spinning in a circle. "I was supposed to go left! No, right! Wait, which way is right? And which is left?" Ari groans, collapsing under a tree and burying his face in his hands.

"This is the worst day ever!"

The crack of twigs makes Ari look up, startled to see an old wizard in a tall, pointed hat, matching cloak, and long, scraggly beard stepping out from behind a tree.

"It can't be all that bad!" the wizard says, leaning on his knotted walking stick.

"Who are you?" Ari's heart thumps hard in his chest.

"I'm a wizard, obviously!" he says brightly, standing beside Ari. "The real question is, who are *you*?"

Ari shrugs. "I'm just a kid having the worst day ever."

"The worst day ever?" the wizard is surprised. "That can't be true."

"It is!" Ari says. "Not a single good thing happened today."

"Meeting a magical wizard in the woods isn't a good thing?" the wizard chuckles. "Even when all seems lost, there are things to be grateful for."

"I guess," Ari says, unconvinced. Then he takes a deep breath and lets it out slowly. "The weather is kind of nice today," he shrugs. "And it was pizza day in the cafeteria."

"Tell me, is today still the worst day ever?" asks the wizard.

Chapter 4 Activities

Activity 1: Thank You Card Writing
Activity Type: Worksheet

Activity 2: Silver Lining Craft Project
Activity Type: Craft

Activity 3: The Best Part of My Day
Activity Type: Discussion

Activity 4: A Kind Place
Activity Type: Class worksheet

Extension 1: Gratitude Wall
Activity Type: Craft

Extension 2: Thank You Card Design Challenge
Activity Type: Art

continued next page

SEL Vocabulary

appreciate [verb]: to understand the true value or worth of something

gratitude [noun]: the feeling we get when we choose to notice the good things in our lives

perspective [noun]: the way we look at something, our point of view

support people [noun]: the people in our lives who are ready to help us when us can't do it alone

visual representation [noun]: an image that shows something that you can't usually see

Lost In The Park
continued

Ari thinks about this. "I guess it's not all bad. I'm still lost, though."

"Can I help you find your way?"

"I already tried following a map but still got lost," replies Ari miserably.

"Did you know," the wizard says, "that some of the greatest explorers in history didn't always have a map?"

Ari says doubtfully, "Then how did they find their way?"

"They used the stars," the wizard answers, grinning.

"It's daytime," Ari points at the clear blue sky. "No stars."

"Oh really?" the old wizard has a mischievous smile. He taps the end of his walking stick on the ground three times. "Look at your hands."

Ari looks down at his hands, first in confusion and then in wonder. On his right hand, three tiny red stars have appeared. And on his left, there are three lime green stars to match.

"Ruby red for right, lime green for left!" Ari says excitedly.

"We wizards call that *a visual representation*. And don't worry, it'll wash off. Now, all you have to do," says the wizard, "is go straight down to the river, then take a Ruby Red. After that, go straight again, and then the ball field will be on the Lime Green side."

"Take a ruby red right at the river," Ari repeats, "and the ball field will be on my lime green left."

Ari thanks the wizard and heads off. Soon, he is at the ball field. And he's just in time for the last inning!

Despite missing most of the game, Ari feels grateful. He has learned a helpful new trick for telling right from left. All it took was getting lost and a little help from a wizard.

56   Chapter: 4 Gratitude

ACTIVITY OVERVIEW
Activity 1: Thank You Card Writing

OBJECTIVE
Students will write a message of gratitude to someone important in their life using sentence frames to help them organize their thoughts.

MATERIALS
- ✓ Thank You Card Template (downloadable PDF)
- ✓ Writing and coloring utensils
- ✓ Optional: envelopes and postage

PROMPT

Think of a time when someone thanked you because you did something meaningful for them. How did you feel when they showed their gratitude?

Today, we will share our gratitude for someone we appreciate. Sometimes, it can be tricky to find the right words. So, we have a fill-in-the-blank thank you card to help us get started.

PROCEDURE
- Have students think of someone they want to express gratitude to. Each student can fill in the blanks in the printable thank you card. Students who need support with writing can use a scribe. The priority is to capture their words as they express them verbally.
- Once they have completed the message, students can spend the remainder of their time drawing an image in the box on the front of the card to decorate it if they choose to.
- Students may choose to send their cards to the recipient.

CLOSURE

Closing discussion questions:
- How did you feel as you made the card?
- How would your recipient feel if they read your card?

CHAPTER 4: Gratitude | ACTIVITY 1: Thank You Card Writing

Thank You Card Template

Dear _____,

Thank you for _____
_____.

It always makes me feel _____
when you _____.
_____ is really special to me.

I love when _____.

_____

ACTIVITY OVERVIEW
Activity 2: Silver Lining Craft Project

OBJECTIVE
Students will practice focusing on gratitude when faced with a challenging situation.

MATERIALS
- ✓ Writing or drawing utensils that will show up on dark paper
- ✓ Construction paper in two colors, one dark, one light

PROMPT

Gratitude can help us when we are feeling overwhelmed and upset. Have you ever heard the phrase "What's the silver lining?" Looking for the silver lining means taking a frustrating situation and finding some part of it—even a small part—that is positive.

Today, we will complete a craft that will helps us practice finding the silver lining in our "dark, bad-day" clouds.

While we feel upset, finding gratitude can lighten our mood by reminding us that things can still make us smile even when we are in a difficult situation. We might not stop feeling upset, but we can still make room for the good stuff!

PROCEDURE
- Find an image online showing a cloud with a silver lining. Ask students to make observations about the picture. Introduce the idea that a silver lining can highlight the positive side of a difficult situation.
- Ask the students to find a silver lining for the sample scenarios below or come up with more relevant scenarios for your students.
    - It's raining on the day you were planning to go to the park.
    - You lost your favorite item (pencil, toy, etc.).
    - Your teacher gave you a really hard assignment.
- Have students draw and cut out a cloud shape from the dark paper. This is their "dark, bad-day" cloud. Invite students to write or draw the difficult situation they face on the cloud.
- Next, have students place their cloud shape on top of a sheet of lighter-colored paper and trace around the edge with roughly an inch margin. Then, students can cut out the larger cloud shape and glue it onto the back of their dark cloud.
- Finally, prompt students to write or draw the good things that are also true along the edge of the lighter cloud.

CLOSURE

Invite volunteers to share their crafts. Prompt them to highlight their favorite part of their work with the group.

Closing discussion questions:

- What were the silver linings you found for the scenario?
- What was it like to look for silver linings? Was it easy? Challenging? Why?

The Teacher's Toolbox For Every Child

ACTIVITY OVERVIEW

Activity 3: The Best Part of My Day

OBJECTIVE
Students will practice reflecting on the positive parts of their day.

MATERIALS
- ✓ Optional: A ball or special object to serve as a symbol of whose turn it is to speak.

PROMPT

We all experience both hard things and fun things each day. Let us take a moment to reflect on the best thing that happened on a day this week or that's happened to you today.

It could be something you did, a friend did, something that happened to you, or something you saw that brought you positive feelings.

PROCEDURE

- Have students stand or sit in a circle and go around from student to student, allowing each to share one good thing from their day. Students should be allowed to pass if they don't feel like sharing. Teachers can model by going first.

Modification

For students who have difficulty staying quiet during turn-taking activities, it may be helpful to use some sort of special object that can mark whose turn it is to speak. This can be anything you want, so long as it feels meaningful to the students.

CLOSURE

Thank students for sharing about their days.

Quick Tip: This simple and quick activity can be effective as a regular classroom practice. There are lots of ways to turn this activity into a special routine that students look forward to:

- **Add a movement component!** Have students toss or roll a ball around the circle as they share, or pair the activity with a game of freeze dance allowing one to three children to share during each freeze.
- **Make it a transition!** Ask students to share their reflection before being dismissed from a group activity into independent work.
- **Use shares to help build connection with your students.** This activity is a great way to learn more about their interests and lives outside of school.

ACTIVITY OVERVIEW
Activity 4: A Kind Place

OBJECTIVE
Students will work together as a class to practice offering acts of kindness to one another.

MATERIALS
✓ Acts of Kindness Log (downloadable PDF)

PROMPT
One of the best ways to help ourselves feel grateful is by sharing our gratitude with others. Over the next week, we will play a game where our classroom will become a Kind Place. This means we will try to see how many acts of kindness we can do as a group. At the end of each day, we will see how many acts of kindness we completed and try to beat our record from the day before.

PROCEDURE
- Pin up the Acts of Kindness Log somewhere visible and easily accessible for the students.
- Review how to fill out an entry as a group. Make predictions as a class about how many entries the students think they can record.
- Set one to three moments in the day when you can prompt students to add to the log. If possible, make it an option to add to the log unprompted during other appropriate moments.
- At the end of the day, compare how many entries the class logged compared with their predictions. Was it more or less? Were they surprised?

Modification
Continue the activity for one-week or longer: You can keep this activity going as long as it interests and motivates students, but a good duration is to continue for about one week.

Set a class goal for the next day or week to beat the number from day one.

CLOSURE
Closing discussion questions:
- How did the feeling of the classroom change while we were creating a kind place together?
- What do you notice about the Acts of Kindness Log? Were all acts of kindness the same? Did all of them have to take a lot of effort?
- In what other ways can we practice kindness that are not already on this list?

The Teacher's Toolbox For Every Child

CHAPTER 4: Gratitude | ACTIVITY 4: A Kind Place
Acts of Kindness Log

Describe your act of kindness:

ACTIVITY OVERVIEW
Extension Activities

EXTENSION 1:

Gratitude Wall

Print Gratitude Wall printable from the downloadable PDF file.

Ask students to record their sharing from "Best Part of My Day" activity on the printable hearts. They can color or decorate their hearts as they choose.

Create a display of the hearts on a bulletin board or wall to create a visual reminder of all the good things.

EXTENSION 2:

Thank You Card Design Challenge

Have students create a thank you card using words or images that convey a sense of gratitude.

Students can choose their preferred medium: drawing, painting, or collage to create their cards. Teachers can show sample thank you card images to help spur students' creativity.

IDEAS & NOTES

_____
_____
_____
_____
_____
_____
_____
_____
_____

CHAPTER 4: Gratitude | EXTENSION 1: Gratitude Wall

Gratitude Wall

Name: _____ Date: _____

Chapter 5:
Curiosity

Discussion Guide

READ ALOUD OBJECTIVE
Students will consider how following their curiosities leads them to think creatively and find new ways to solve problems.

STORY SUMMARY
Dylan is working on an invention called the Mess-o-Matic 3000. She gives Jamie a demonstration even though the machine hasn't been finished. When the test run ends in disaster, Dylan is still excited and curious to explore all the new information she got from the experiment.

COMPREHENSION QUESTIONS

1. What is the machine that Dylan is building supposed to do?
   Answer: It's supposed to make her homework neat.

2. Why did Dylan try a test of the Mess-o-Matic 3000 even though she knew it wasn't finished?
   Answer: Dylan was curious about what would happen.

3. What happened when Dylan put Jamie's homework into the Mess-o-Matic 3000?
   Answer: The machine blew up.

READ ALOUD INTRODUCTION
Today, we will read a story about an inventor, Dylan, who uses her curiosity to invent something unique. Except it doesn't go exactly the way she planned. Curiosity is the feeling we get when we want to know more about something. While reading the story, think about what the inventor does that shows she is curious.

READ ALOUD CLOSURE
Curiosity is a trait that helps us think creatively and solve problems. Dylan's curiosity not only helped her come up with the idea for the Mess-o-Matic 3000 but also helped her to get right back into it after the explosion!

LISTEN TO THE AUDIO VERSION OF THE STORY

DISCUSSION QUESTIONS

1. Why is Dylan creating the Mess-o-Matic 3000?

2. Was Dylan upset after the Mess-o-Matic 3000 blew up? Why or why not?

3. Can you think of a time when you felt so curious that you tried experimenting or building something just like Dylan did?

Chapter: 5 Curiosity

READ ALOUD:
The Mess-o-Matic 3000

"What in the world is that thing?" Jamie called from across the workshop to where Dylan was tightening a screw on a mysterious-looking machine.

"When this beauty is done…" said Dylan with a grunt as she gave a final twist with the screwdriver, "no one will be able to tell me my homework is too messy again."

Jamie shot Dylan a skeptical look. "For real?"

"For real," Dylan confirmed, jiggling a wire until one of the many tubes on top of the machine started flashing green. "I was daydreaming about how cool it would be if I could invent something that made my homework look neat for me since my teacher always comments on my messy work. Then, I got curious about how to design it. And soon I just had to see if I could actually build it! Now, I have to make a few last adjustments, and the Homework-o-Matic 3000 will be ready to go!"

Dylan stepped back as the clunky contraption began to whir and hum. It had taken hours of tinkering to calibrate the algorithms.

"No way!" said Jamie, coming closer to get a better look at the enormous machine. "That's too good to be true. Can you show me how it works?"

Dylan took a deep breath. "Sure! I'm curious to find out what happens in a test run myself. Here's yesterday's messy homework."

Dylan placed the paper in the slot at the top of the machine and pressed a few buttons. "We'll set it to super neat mode and press start."

The friends watched eagerly as the machine whirred, pulling the paper inside. Then the machine clanked, rumbled, and let out what sounded like a giant burp!

"Excuse you," giggled Jamie as the machine clicked and thrummed until it shook so hard it looked like it was jumping on the worktable. All at once, great puffs of smoke poured out of the slot where the homework had gone in, and the air smelled like burnt marshmallows.

"It's overheating!" shouted Dylan.

"It's going to blow!" yelled Jamie.

The kids ducked just in time. A loud bang followed another loud burping sound, and sprockets, springs, screws, and wires started flying in every direction. Finally, with a disgusting sound, the machine spewed out a storm of green slime.

continued next page

Chapter 5 Activities

Activity 1: **Active Listening Game**
Activity Type: Game

Activity 2: **Design It Your Way**
Activity Type: Design

Activity 3: **Self-Discovery Writing**
Activity Type: Writing

Activity 4: **Research Scavenger Hunt**
Activity Type: Research

Extension 1: **Self-Discovery Poem**
Activity Type: Writing

Extension 2: **Create a New Class**
Activity Type: Design

The Mess-o-Matic 3000
continued

"I think the Mess-o-Matic 3000 failed its test run," Jamie said as he stepped carefully through the wreckage of Dylan's hard work.

Dylan's eyes lit up as she tapped her chin, deep in thought. "It didn't fail! It just gave me even more things to be curious about!"

"It did?" Jamie asked, nudging a fallen spring with the toe of his shoe. "It looks like all it gave you was an even bigger mess."

Dylan began picking up the pieces. "If the machine is overheated, there must be an issue with the algebraic cooling system. Maybe I can adjust the conversion system to give the organization network more power!"

"I'll come back for the next test run," Jaime said. "See you later!"

But Dylan didn't answer. She was already happily working to put her machine back together, flipping through an engineering manual curiously searching for the solution to her problem.

SEL Vocabulary

active listening [noun]: engaging with what someone is saying through asking questions, summarizing what they have said, and imagining what they might be implying with their tone and body language

attention deficit hyperactivity disorder (ADHD) [noun]: a term used by teachers and doctors to talk about how some students learn best when they get extra support to stay focused on their work during the school day. This is especially hard when they feel that the work is boring, or when they think the work will take a long time to finish. Without support, these students also find it hard to keep track of their belongings and they may also have lots of energy in their bodies and find it really hard to sit in a way that's expected at school.

curiosity [noun]: the desire to understand something that still needs to be clarified

dyscalculia [noun]: a term used by teachers and doctors to talk about how some students learn best when they get extra support to help them understand their math work. Without support, these students can struggle to understand what they're supposed to do with math problems. They can have trouble doing math in their minds, memorizing math facts, understanding the difference between greater than and less than, putting numbers in order, and making sense of word problems. So even things like adding and subtracting become really hard for them.

dyslexia [noun]: a term used by teachers and doctors to talk about how some students learn best when they get extra support connecting letters with the sounds that they make. Without help, these students can struggle to recognize letters and words they already learned and have a hard time figuring out new words. They can have a difficult time reading smoothly and make lots of errors in their spelling and writing work.

learning differences (LD) [noun]: a term used by teachers and doctors to talk about all of the different ways that kids may need extra support at school, including dyslexia and dyscalculia.

perspective [noun]: the way each person sees the world differently based on their experiences, knowledge, and values

self-reflection [noun]: being curious about our own thoughts and actions

ACTIVITY OVERVIEW

Activity 1: Active Listening Game

OBJECTIVE
Students will practice asking thoughtful questions utilizing active listening and critical thinking to help them determine the correct answer in each round of this engaging and silly game.

MATERIALS
✓ Active Listening Word Bank (downloadable PDF)

Modification
For younger students, finding the answer within 20 questions may be challenging. You can give students a category to pick from (animals, vehicles, objects in the classroom, etc.) to narrow the possibilities.

PROMPT
Curiosity helps us learn new things, develop the skills to solve problems and overcome challenges.

Today, we will play an Active Listening Game where we ask strategic, thoughtful questions to exercise this skill.

PROCEDURE
- In each turn, students may choose their own secret words or pick from the choices in the Active Listening Word Bank provided.
  - The teacher or one student is the Secret Keeper and picks a secret word, then answers other students' questions as they try to guess what the secret word is.
  - The rest of the group are Investigators. They work together, asking the Secret Keeper yes or no questions until they figure out the secret word.
  - The goal is to develop thoughtful and strategic questions so we can guess the secret word within 20 questions. If we can't get it right in that many questions, the Secret Keeper will reveal the word.
- For each question, translate the response into a statement on the board. This will help students connect the power of their inquiry to the information gathered.
  - Question: Is your secret word a person?
  - Answer: No
  - Clue: We know that the word is not human!
- Turn-taking: To ensure equitable participation in larger groups, going around the class in order may be helpful.

CLOSURE
Closing discussion questions:
- What kind of questions gave us the most critical information?
- How did summarizing the information we gathered on the board help us to ask better questions?
- After playing this game, what have you learned about curiosity?

CHAPTER 5: Curiosity | ACTIVITY 1: Active Listening Game

Active Listening Word Bank

Ice cream	T-Rex	Book	Truck	Fish
Bike	Rabbit	Baseball bat	Pig	Bus
Snowman	Trash	Nail polish	French fries	Egg
Gloves	Jump rope	Hammer	Cat	Backpack
Gum	Wagon	Duck	Hat	The Moon
Train	Skates	Drums	Ball	Glasses
Bug	Bird	Rain	Volcano	Cup
Hand	Rug	Puppy	House	Soap

Copyright © SuperDville

ACTIVITY OVERVIEW
Activity 2: Design It Your Way

OBJECTIVE
Open-ended questions help us explore areas we are curious about. It's also a great way to practice conversation skills! In small groups, students will explore open-ended questions about their lives at school. Then, they will use their chosen medium to record their thoughts and ideas.

MATERIALS
✓ Paper
✓ Drawing utensils

PROMPT
In the story, "The Mess-o-Matic 3000," Dylan uses her curiosity and imagination to create a machine. Dylan is an inventor, so her imagination led her to an invention.

Today, we will use our curiosity and imagination to answer questions about school. You can write a story, draw a picture, or even write a song in response to the question you choose.

PROCEDURE
- Break students into groups of 2-3 and give each group a question from the list below:
    - Imagine you are the principal for the day. What are the first two things you would do?
    - What are some new subjects you think should be added to school? Why do you think kids need to learn about them?
    - What would the perfect playground look like?
    - How do you think school will be different in 100 years?
    - Think of the best part of the school day. What would make it even better?
    - If you could, how would you arrange our daily class schedule?
- Allow students 5 minutes to brainstorm and 10-15 minutes to design. Prompt them to show their ideas using pictures, words, or an idea map.

Modification
Increase student engagement by allowing them to choose the question they want to work on. Write each question on a large piece of paper at different tables throughout the classroom. Let kids walk around and then decide where to sit.

CLOSURE
Once students complete their designs, each group can share their ideas with the class.

Closing discussion questions:
- What is your favorite idea from your group discussion?
- What questions do you have about what the other groups did?

ACTIVITY OVERVIEW
Activity 3: Self-Discovery Writing

OBJECTIVE

Students will engage in self-discovery through an automatic writing challenge. With each new sentence, they will discover new things about themselves.

MATERIALS
- ✓ Lined paper
- ✓ Writing utensils
- ✓ Optional - ball

PROMPT

One way to be curious is to look out at the world and wonder why things are the way they are. Another way to be curious is to wonder and ask questions about ourselves. This is called self-discovery.

Today, we will practice turning our curiosity inward by completing the sentence "I'm proud of..." We will repeatedly find different ways we can finish this sentence.

We don't have to worry about our handwriting or correct spelling. Our goal is to find as many different ways as possible to complete the sentence. You might even be surprised by some of your answers!

PROCEDURE

- Write the following sentences on the board and then read them aloud:
    - I'm proud of...
    - My favorite thing about me is...
    - I'm happiest when...
- Ask the students to think about some different ways they could finish each sentence. With younger students it may be useful to spend a few minutes brainstorming ideas as a group. Ask students to write down as many different endings for each sentence as they can come up with.
- Allow 3-5 minutes, depending on the group's tolerance for writing quietly. You can play music, dim the lights, or modify the environment to encourage quiet reflection.

Modification

This can be a one-on-one verbal activity for students who may not prefer writing. The teacher and student can toss a ball back and forth. Each time the student catches the ball, they say the sentence frame with a different response.

CLOSURE

Invite volunteers to share their writing. Prompt them to highlight their favorite part of their work with the group.

The Teacher's Toolbox For Every Child 73

ACTIVITY OVERVIEW
Activity 4: Research Scavenger Hunt

OBJECTIVE
Kids will use the internet to gather information about famous people with learning differences throughout history.

MATERIALS
✓ Research Scavenger Hunt (downloadable PDF)

PROMPT
You will use your curiosity and research skills for an internet scavenger hunt. You'll be searching for famous or accomplished people with learning differences.

Many people process information differently or have sensory processing issues and have used their creative minds to accomplish amazing things. Your challenge today is to use your curiosity and inquiry skills to find them!

PROCEDURE
- Complete the Research Challenge sheet individually or in pairs.

Modification
For groups with less exposure to technology, it may be helpful to go over the best search terms. You can recommend phrases like "famous scientists with learning differences."

Encourage students to experiment with their search terms, using specific learning differences (ADHD, dyslexia, dyscalculia, etc.) and the word "disabilities," as these words are used to describe learning differences. This is a powerful way to normalize learning differences by using accurate terminology.

CLOSURE
Closing discussion questions:
- Who was the most interesting or surprising person you found in your research?
- What did you learn about them that you will remember the most?

CHAPTER 5: Curiosity | ACTIVITY 4: Research Scavenger Hunt
Research Scavenger Hunt

Name: _____ Date: _____

Circle the profession that most interests you. Use your research skills to find a famous person with learning differences in that career. Draw or write the important things you learn about them in the box.

Scientist	Actor	Athlete
Writer	Entrepreneur	Musician
Gamer	Artist	Chef

If you could talk to the person you found, what is the first question you would ask them? _____

_____

_____

ACTIVITY OVERVIEW
Extension Activities

EXTENSION 1:
Self-Discovery Poem

Convert Your Self-Discovery Writing into a poem. Have students read their writing aloud to themselves and create a second draft in the form of a poem.

Student volunteers can be invited to read their poems to the class. They can also choose a friend to be their reader if reading aloud is something they prefer not to do. This should be a person the student chooses themselves and can be a friend or even the teacher.

EXTENSION 2:
Create a New Class

Students think of a topic they are curious about and come up with five questions they would want to explore. They can pretend to be a teacher who teaches a class on this topic. What would you name this class, and what other details would you want students to learn?

Some possible topics are a class about:

- Advanced Study of Clowning
- Introduction to Skateboarding
- Communicating with Your Pet

IDEAS & NOTES

_____
_____
_____
_____
_____
_____
_____
_____
_____
_____

Chapter 6:
Self-Acceptance

Discussion Guide

READ ALOUD OBJECTIVE
Students will learn about embracing their differences. Just because a brain functions differently because a person has dyslexia, ADHD, or some other learning difference, it doesn't mean that person is any less intelligent than someone who doesn't have a learning difference.

STORY SUMMARY
Ariana worries that her dyslexia makes her less intelligent. She wonders if she would be smarter if she had a non-dyslexic brain. The Super D! Kids ask Professor Boom to help use science to prove to Ariana that all brains are different, but that doesn't make one smarter than another.

READ ALOUD INTRODUCTION
Sometimes, the things that make us different give us an obvious advantage. When a difference gives an advantage that others can see, one might get lots of positive feedback. If we're super tall, we'll be able to reach things that others can't. If we're great at singing, we may get the lead in a school musical.

But what if the difference isn't that obvious? For example, what if we have a learning difference, like dyslexia? We might think that this sort of difference doesn't have its advantages. In fact, we might wish the difference didn't exist.

We will read a story today about a girl who thinks that having dyslexia means she is not as smart as her friends who aren't dyslexic. As we read, think about what being different means to you.

READ ALOUD CLOSURE
Ariana's dyslexia means that the way she has learned certain things such as reading may be different from people who don't have dyslexia. It does not mean she is less intelligent.

LISTEN TO THE AUDIO VERSION OF THE STORY

COMPREHENSION QUESTIONS

1. **Why is Ariana feeling down?**
   Answer: She worries that having dyslexia means that she is less intelligent.

2. **How does Professor Boom compare the dyslexic and non-dyslexic brains?**
   Answer: Professor Boom feels, examines, and listens to the brains.

3. **What do we learn from Professor Boom's experiment?**
   Answer: All brains are different. That is one of the things that makes us all special and unique.

DISCUSSION QUESTIONS

1. Do you find talking about what makes you different easy or hard? Why or why not?

2. Why do you think people feel shy about discussing the things that make them different?

3. Can you think of anything that makes you unique that you feel proud about?

READ ALOUD:
Professor Boom and the Dyslexic Brain

Ellie and Lexi, during an after-school club for kids with dyslexia, are relaxing in the rec room before they start on their homework.

A *ding-ding* sound chimes from the rec room computer letting the girls know that they have a new video message to watch.

"Hi, Super D! Friends. I'm Ariana, and I'm dyslexic," the girl on the screen says. "Sometimes I wish I had a non-dyslexic brain because I don't always feel smart. Do you think a non-dyslexic brain would make me smarter?"

"Wow," Lexi frowns as the video comes to an end. "That's really sad that Ariana feels that way about being dyslexic."

"Yeah," Ellie agrees, "Being dyslexic doesn't mean you're not smart."

"I wish there was a way we could prove that to Ariana," Lexi says. She frowns as she thinks until a big smile comes over her face. "Wait, maybe there is."

"Let's call Professor Boom!" the friends say at the same time.

"She'll know what to do!" Lexi says as she video calls Professor Boom on the computer.

Moments later, Professor Boom is on the screen. The kids explain the situation, and she is shocked.

"Hudson!" Professor Boom calls to someone offscreen, "We have an emergency. It's time to fetch... the brains!"

A moment later, Professor Boom's assistant, Hudson, appears, carrying a tray holding two wiggly, jiggly brains.

"The dyslexic brain is super smart, and I can prove it," Professor Boom says into the camera.

"But how?" Lexi asks.

"By comparing these two brains!" Professor Boom answers.

In front of one of the brains is a label reading *Dyslexic Brain*. In front of the other, the label reads *Non-Dyslexic Brain*.

Professor Boom snaps on her gloves. Then, she grabs the non-dyslexic brain and examines it closely, turning it over and over and over again. "I see," she whispers, setting the brain down.

continued next page

Chapter 6 Activities

Activity 1: **Self-Love Self-Portrait**
Activity Type: Art Project

Activity 2: **Affirmation Mirror**
Activity Type: Community Building Exercise

Activity 3: **Every Side of Me Accordion Book**
Activity Type: Craft

Activity 4: **Every Brain Is Different**
Activity Type: Worksheet

Extension 1: **Mirror Talk 3 x 3**
Activity Type: Improvisation

Extension 2: **Journal Prompt**
Activity Type: Writing

SEL Vocabulary

judgment [noun]: deciding whether the way others act is good and bad

neurodiversity [noun]: the idea that the networks inside of human brains can be organized in different ways and there can be benefits and challenges to each

self-acceptance [noun]: the act or state of recognizing and accepting one's own abilities and limitations

self-compassion [noun]: a self-attitude involving treating oneself with love and understanding, even in difficult times

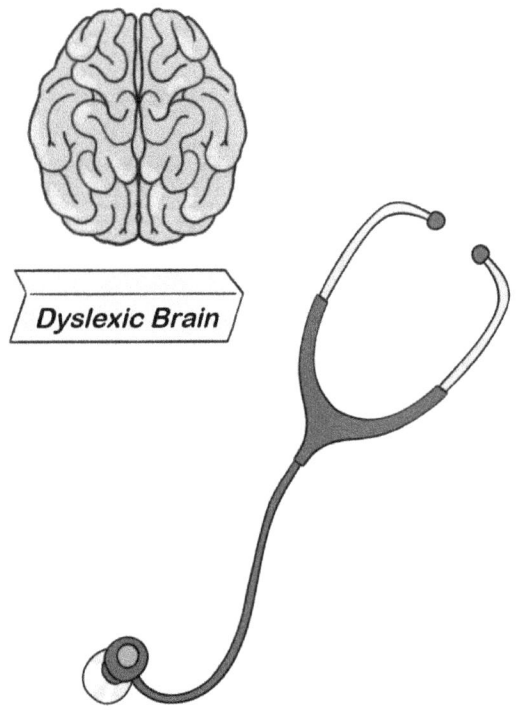

Dyslexic Brain

Professor Boom and the Dyslexic Brain
continued

Professor Boom moves on to examine the dyslexic brain. She picks it up and peers at it, whispering, "Interesting. Hudson! Write this down!"

Hudson eagerly picks up his clipboard and pencil.

"Both brains are gooey, slimy, and wet," Professor Boom says. "And they have the same color and texture. So now we know that both brains feel and look the same."

Hudson takes notes as the professor continues. "But we need to do one more test to put Ariana's mind at ease. We must LISTEN to the brains," declares Professor Boom. She presses the end of her stethoscope to the non-dyslexic brain.

"Wow!" she shouts. "The non-dyslexic brain sounds organized. A very rhythmic song–like a marching band!" Then, she quickly moves to listen to the dyslexic brain. "Another wow!" she shouts. "It sounds incredible as well! The dyslexic brain sounds different, changing, and unpredictable, like a drum solo."

With a proud smile, Professor Boom takes off her stethoscope. "That settles it, Hudson! I FELT the brains, I EXAMINED the brains, and I LISTENED to the brains! Both are intelligent and do their job in their own way!"

Back in the rec room, Ellie and Lexi cheer as Professor Boom shares her findings on both brains.

"So the brains look the same, but they have different ways of thinking," Ellie says.

"And thank goodness for that!" Professor Boom says. "Imagine if every brain thought the same way? If everyone had the same creative ideas or solutions to problems?"

"The world would be pretty boring," Lexi says.

"Those who think differently due to conditions like dyslexia add to the neurodiversity of the world," Professor Boom says before ending the video call.

Next, Lexi and Ellie send Ariana a video message of their own. Their message begins, "Your dyslexic brain is AMAZING!"

ACTIVITY OVERVIEW
Activity 1: Self-Love Self-Portrait

OBJECTIVE
Students will reflect on the characteristics they love about themselves.

MATERIALS
- ✓ Photograph or drawing of each child
- ✓ Construction paper
- ✓ Crayons, pencils, colored pencils, or markers
- ✓ Optional: Other art materials

PROMPT

In the story "Professor Boom and the Dyslexic Brain," Ariana is feeling bad about being different. Professor Boom shows her that different doesn't mean bad.

Today, we will make art inspired by the things that make us different and show how wonderful these parts of ourselves are.

PROCEDURE

- Have each child cut out the image of themselves and glue it onto a piece of construction paper. For kids who struggle with fine motor skills, teachers may want to have the pictures cut out in advance.
- Ask students to think of five to ten traits that make them who they are. Some kids may find this challenging. Teachers can scaffold this activity by writing the following prompts on the board:
  - What skill do you have that is special or unique to you?
  - Is there anything you love or are interested in that you can share with your friends and community?
  - When do you feel the happiest?
  - What makes you different? How do these things help you or give you special skills?
- Ask students to draw pictures, symbols, and words on their construction paper to create a background that depicts these unique parts of their personality and interests.

CLOSURE

Invite volunteers to share their portraits. Prompt them to highlight their favorite part of their work with the group.

ACTIVITY OVERVIEW
Activity 2: Affirmation Mirror

OBJECTIVE
Students will create a positive space in the classroom for self-affirmations.

MATERIALS
- ✓ Shatterproof mirror
- ✓ Pencils, crayons, colored pencils, or markers
- ✓ Post-its

PROMPT

An important way we can help ourselves learn and grow is to speak to ourselves with kindness. In the story "Professor Boom and the Dyslexic Brain," Ariana doesn't view her dyslexia as a strength. In fact, she seems to view it as a weakness.

Today, we will create an Affirmation Mirror. It will be a positive space in our classroom for reminding ourselves of our love and care for ourselves and each other. When we need to be lifted up, anyone in class can visit the space and pick out some kind words to say to themselves in our new affirmation mirror.

PROCEDURE

- Hang the mirror on the wall before the start of the lesson in a place with enough space to add the Post-it notes around the edge, and so students visiting the mirror will have enough room to take a quiet moment when they need it. If the classroom has a quiet corner, that is an excellent place for the Affirmation Mirror.

- Write the following affirmations on the board as examples.
  - You are brave!
  - You are so much fun to be around!
  - You are a great problem solver!

- Pass out Post-it notes to all the children in the class. Ask them to think of kind words they would like to say to a friend using the phrases on the board as examples. Challenge each kid to think of one to three phrases.

- When each student has finished, invite them to stick their Post-its around the mirror's frame. While in front of the mirror, invite them to choose a note and say the words on it to their reflection.

CLOSURE

Closing discussion questions:

- What was your favorite affirmation phrase? Why did you like it?
- What was it like to say those words to yourself in the mirror?
- When would you want to use the affirmation mirror during the school day?

ACTIVITY OVERVIEW
Activity 3: Every Side of Me Accordion Book

OBJECTIVE
In this activity, students will think about what it means to love all parts of themselves.

MATERIALS
✓ The Many Sides of Me (downloadable PDF)
✓ Scissors
✓ Coloring utensils

PROMPT

Each and every person has many parts of their personality that come out during different times. For example, my playful side comes out during recess, when I get to join in a game of hide and seek. Then, if I go to the library, my serious side might come out. It wouldn't make much sense for me to act silly in the library and serious at recess!

Different situations bring out different parts of our personalities, and since each of us has our own unique mix of personality traits, the combinations are endless!

Today, we will create a book that showcases some of our personality traits, and explore how we can appreciate each one.

PROCEDURE
- Have the group brainstorm together some different "sides" of themselves to generate some examples. Some ideas might include:
  - My shy side
  - My goofy side
  - My adventurous side
- Give each student a copy of the Many Sides of Me printable and allow them time to label and color each page. Encourage students to think about what facial expressions will help convey each "side" of themselves.

CLOSURE
Invite volunteers to share their books. Prompt them to highlight their favorite part of their work with the group.

The Teacher's Toolbox For Every Child

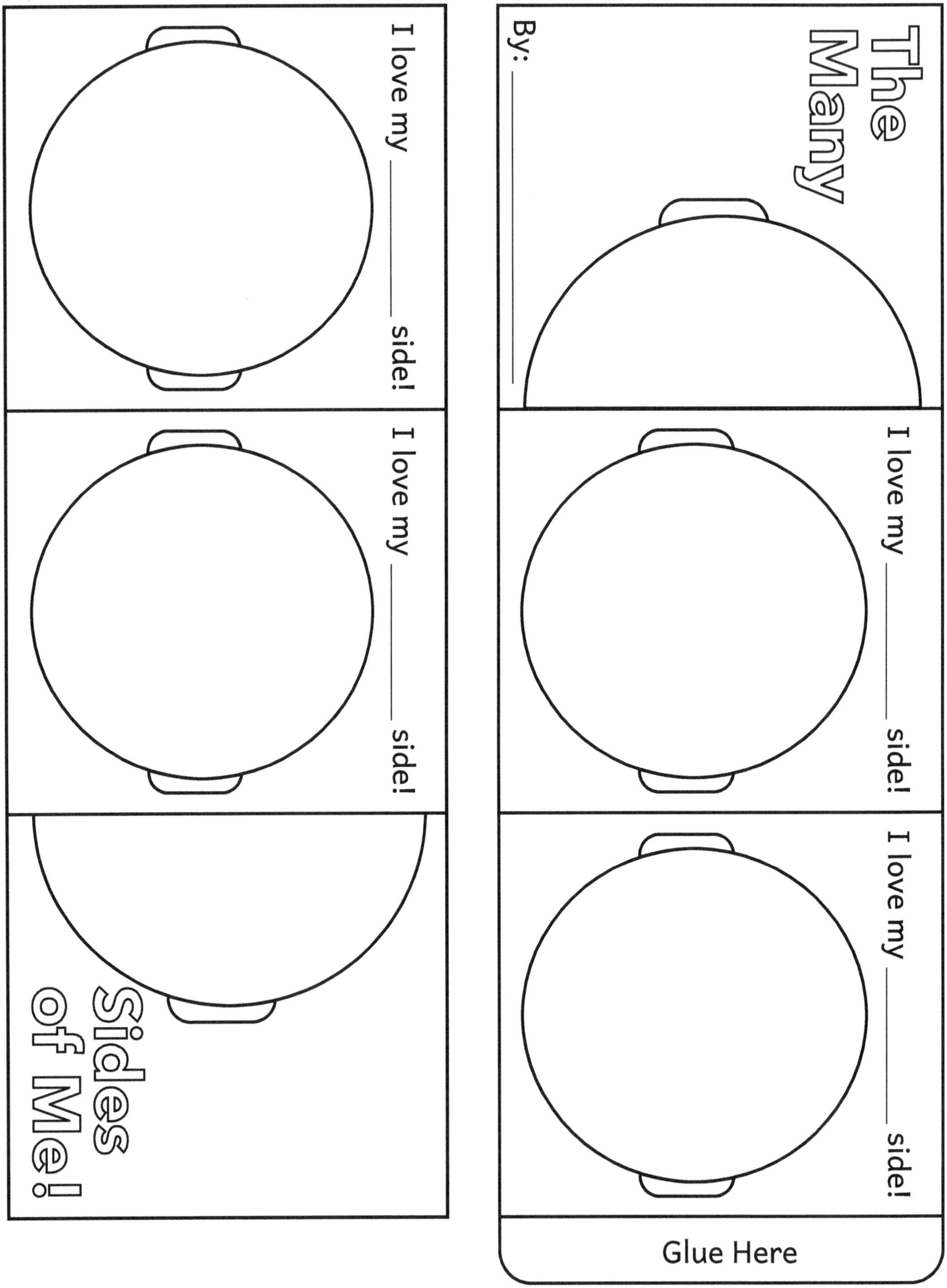

CHAPTER 6: Self-Acceptance | ACTIVITY 3: Every Side of Me Accordion Book

The Many Sides of Me!

By: _____

I love my _____ side!

I love my _____ side!

I love my _____ side!

I love my _____ side!

I love my _____ side!

Glue Here

ACTIVITY OVERVIEW
Activity 4: Every Brain Is Different

OBJECTIVE
Students will explore their own areas of intelligence and notice how their strengths fit in with those of other kids in their classroom.

MATERIALS
- ✓ My Brain Strengths (downloadable PDF)
- ✓ Many Ways to Be Smart (downloadable PDF)
- ✓ Coloring supplies

PROMPT

Did you know that, just like snowflakes and fingerprints, every single brain is unique? Every single person has their own way of processing information and their own way of being intelligent.

Today, we will look at eight areas of specialization, or intelligences, that we will map for ourselves. Then, we will look at our maps together and see what we notice about our class as a group.

PROCEDURE

- Give each student a My Brain Strengths handout. Teachers can either project or read aloud the examples of each specialization from the Many Ways to Be Smart printable.
- Starting in the bottom of each brain, students can color in one, two, or three layers for each skill area. If the examples describe skills the child feels strong and confident with, they can color in all three layers; if the examples are all challenging, they might just color in one. The resulting chart should show both strengths and growth areas for each student.

CLOSURE

Hang up the printables where the students can see them all together. Be prepared to model for students how to talk about differences between the brains using affirmational language and focusing on each child's strengths.

Closing discussion questions:

- Can you find any two brains that have the same profile?
- Who in the class might you go to if you need help writing a song? Who might you go to if you wanted someone to teach you how to do a handstand? What about if you wanted to plan a camping trip?
- Note that these eight specializations are not the only ways to be skilled. What other specializations aren't included on our maps? (Math knowledge, plant and animal knowledge, mechanical/technical knowledge.)

The Teacher's Toolbox For Every Child

CHAPTER 6: Self-Acceptance | ACTIVITY 4: Every Brain Is Different

My Brain Strengths

Name: _____ Date: _____

Each brain has a skill written above. Color the bottom section of the brain if you struggle with the skill listed above. If you're okay at the skill, color the bottom two sections of the brain. Fill in all three sections if the skill is a strength of yours.

Example

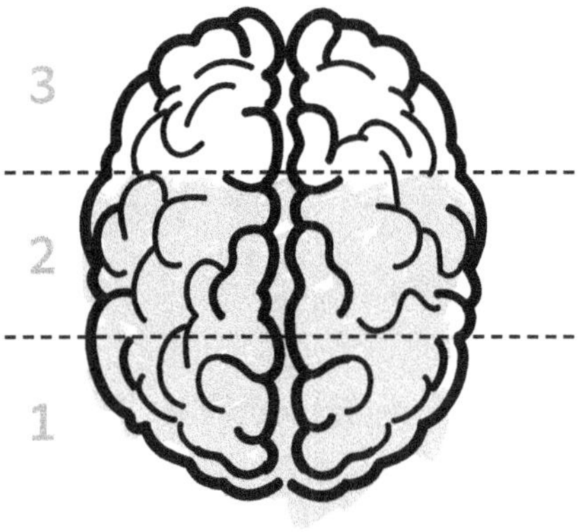

3
2
1

Language Skills

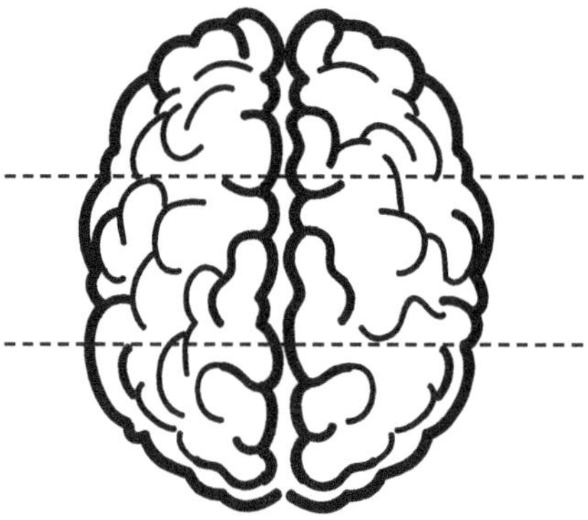

Auditory Skills

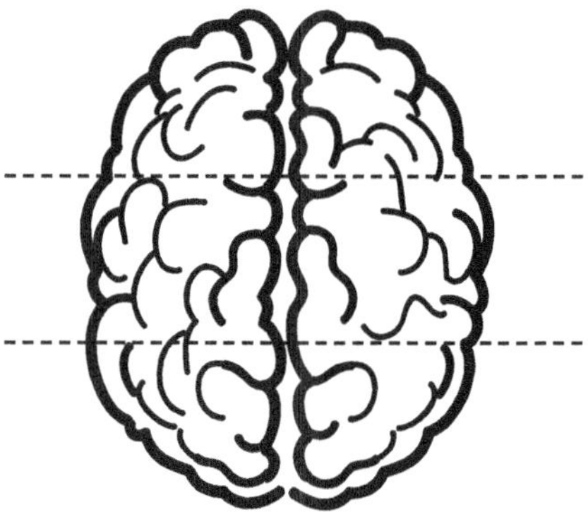

Movement Skills

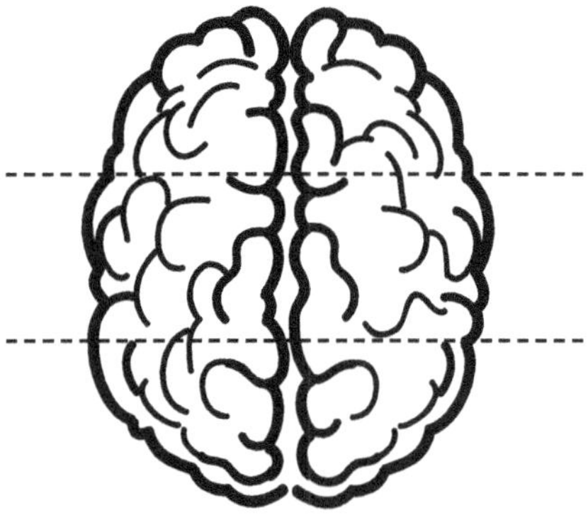

Visual Skills

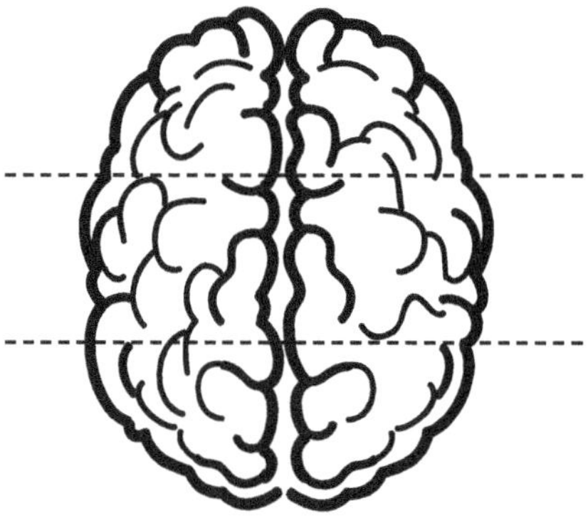

Knowing Myself Skills

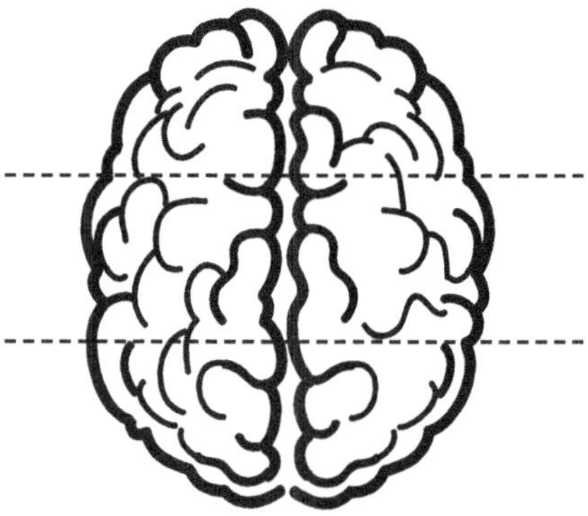

Knowing Others Skills

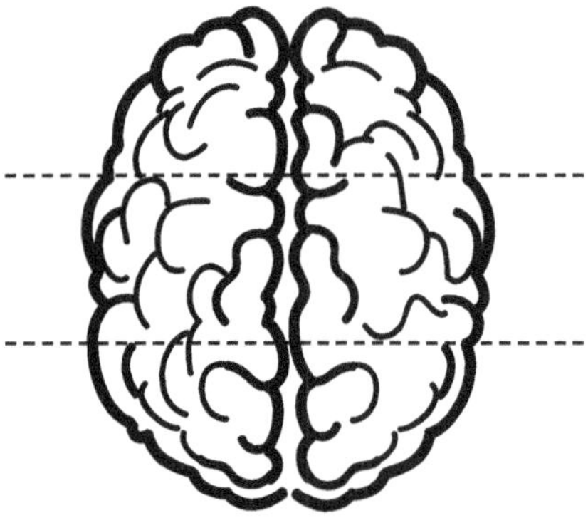

Number Skills

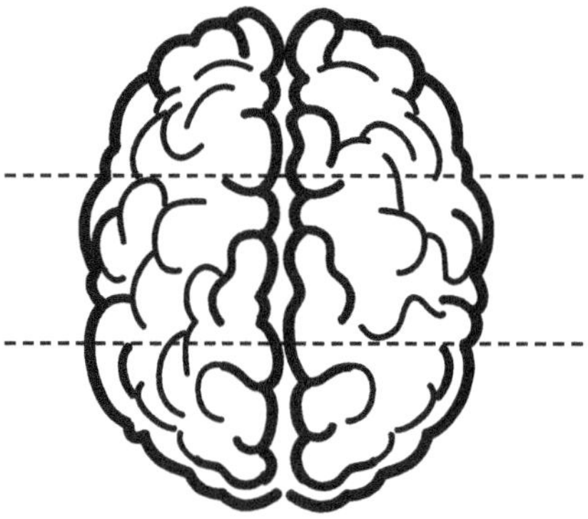

Nature Skills

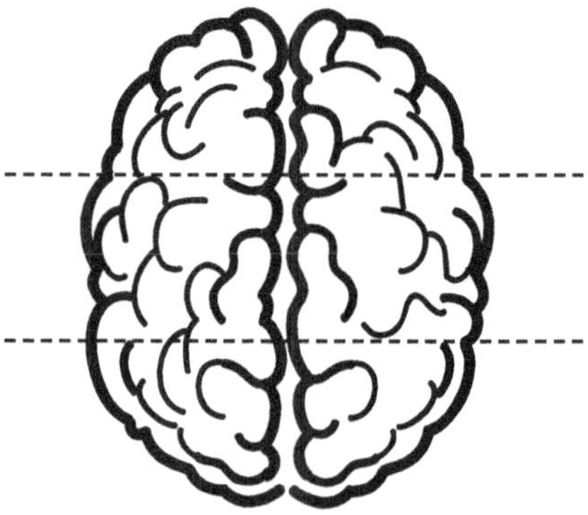

CHAPTER 6: Curiosity | ACTIVITY 4: Every Brain Is Different

Many Ways to Be Smart

Name: _____ Date: _____

Movement skills	playing sports, dancing, having great balance
Seeing skills	fitting a lot in your backpack, making art, solving puzzles
Knowing myself skills	understanding your feelings, knowing your strengths and what's challenging for you
Knowing others skills	making new friends, being able to predict how people will react to a situation, understanding what others are feeling based on their words or body language
Number skills	doing math in your head, estimating, remembering numbers
Nature skills	taking care of plants and animals;, noticing and remembering details in the natural world
Language skills	writing, speech, debate, learning languages, noticing accents, creating new languages
Hearing skills	playing an instrument, singing, memorizing things you hear, remembering songs, distinguishing different instruments when you listen to music

Copyright © SuperDville

ACTIVITY OVERVIEW
Extension Activities

EXTENSION 1:
Mirror Talk 3 by 3

Students pick three affirmations around the mirror to whisper to themselves. They say each phrase aloud three times while looking into their face in the mirror and smiling.

EXTENSION 2:
Journal Prompt

Students can write or make an audio recording to complete this activity. They can choose one trait or interest that makes them different. Then, they can write what they love about that trait. What advantages does it bring? What makes their skill unique and outstanding?

IDEAS & NOTES

_____
_____
_____
_____
_____
_____
_____
_____
_____

Chapter: 6 Self-Acceptance

Chapter 7:
Confidence

Discussion Guide

READ ALOUD OBJECTIVE
Students will reflect on where confidence comes from. They will consider what changed in Jace for him to be able to confront his bullies.

STORY SUMMARY
When Jace is bullied, Pinky, the Guardian Gremlin, gives him a magical hat to boost his confidence. With the hat on, Jace stands up to the bullies and shows them his incredible cello skills. After he surprises the bullies with his confident attitude, his friends help him realize the pink hat is just a regular hat, and he has had that confidence within him all along.

READ ALOUD INTRODUCTION
Confidence is trusting that we can accomplish what we set out to do. Raise your hand if you feel confident you could tell me the words to "Twinkle Twinkle Little Star." Raise your hand if you feel confident you could do a backflip. Okay, that might be a tough one. What if I asked, raise your hand if you feel confident you could *learn* to do a backflip? Raise your hand if you feel confident you can stand up to a bully.

Today, we will read a story about a boy who was bullied. Pay attention to where the main character gets his confidence!

READ ALOUD CLOSURE
Confidence can be tricky because it depends on what we believe about ourselves. This means that the best way to get more confident is to change the stories we tell ourselves about who we are and what we are capable of.

LISTEN TO THE AUDIO VERSION OF THE STORY

COMPREHENSION QUESTIONS

1. **What did Jessica do to make Jace feel upset?**
   Answer: Jessica and her friends made a mean joke about him being in special ed.

2. **How did the Confidence Hat impact Jace?**
   Answer: Wearing the hat made Jace remember what he was good at, which helped him find the courage to stand up to Jessica.

3. **What did Jace realize when he read the tag on the Confidence Hat?**
   Answer: The hat didn't actually have any magical powers. All the hat did was change what Jace believed about himself.

DISCUSSION QUESTIONS

1. Why did Jace show Jessica and the bullies his cello skills when he stood up to them?

2. How do you think Jace felt when he realized the Confidence Hat wasn't actually magical?

3. Can you think of an activity that you feel confident doing?

Chapter: 7 Confidence

READ ALOUD:
Confidence Hat

"Hey guys!" Jace says as he enters the rec room.

"Wow!" Matias says, pausing his ping-pong game with Jordan to take in Jace's bright pink, sparkly hat, "That's a hat-and-a-half!"

"It's my Confidence Hat," Jace says, "And you won't believe where I got it!"

Jordan abandons the game and joins Jace and his giant hat on the couch. "Pink Hats R Us?" Jordan guesses.

"Better," Jace says. "My Guardian Gremlin gave it to me."

"That sounds like a story," Hudson says, taking Jordan's place opposite Matias at the ping-pong table.

"Yeah, spill it," Jordan says.

Jace settles in to share his story, "It happened after school, right after band practice. I was just about to put my cello away when Jessica and her posse stopped me."

"Oof," Matias says, "I bet I know what happened."

He and Hudson stop their game to listen as Jace continues. "And Jessica says, *Hey Jace, did you learn to read today in Special Ed?* And then she and her friends laughed and high-fived each other like it was the funniest joke ever."

"Yeah, it's hilarious to make fun of someone's learning difference," Jordan says dryly.

"And then," Jace says, "right when Jessica and her friends walk away, I open my locker and put my cello away. But just as I closed the locker door, I heard this strange noise, like a wind chime. And then, my locker popped back open, and this little creature sprang out!"

"Creature?" asks Hudson. "Like… a monster?"

"No," Jace says excitedly. "It was little and cute, with pointy ears and wings, and he was dressed entirely in pink!"

"Oo..kay," Hudson says, exchanging a confused glance with Matias and Jordan. "What'd this pink creature say?"

Jace's eyes lit up. "He popped out and said, 'Hello, Jace! How are you today, young sir?' And I said… 'Who are you?' And he said he was Pinky, my magical Guardian Gremlin!"

"*Guardian Gremlin?*" Matias, Jordan, and Hudson gasp.

continued next page

Chapter 7 Activities

Activity 1: **Strengths Bingo**
Activity Type: Game

Activity 2: **Best Friend Voice**
Activity Type: Worksheet

Activity 3: **Comfort Zone Challenge**
Activity Type: Worksheet

Activity 4: **Listening Circle**
Activity Type: Discussion

Extension 1: **Create Your Own Strengths Bingo Card**
Activity Type: Worksheet

Extension 2: **Stretch Zone Challenge**
Activity Type: Group Share

SEL Vocabulary

confidence [noun]: the feeling of trust in oneself that one has the skills or traits needed to do something

inner critic [noun]: the voice in our own mind that tells us unkind words and ideas about ourselves. In this chapter we call it the "bully voice."

negative self-talk [noun]: when the brain tells stories about us that make us question our abilities

positive self-talk [noun]: when the brain makes us believe in our abilities

self-esteem [noun]: the feeling of calm and happiness when we like who we are as a person

Confidence Hat
continued

"Exactly," Jace confirmed. "Pinky said I looked sad, and I told him I was fine, but really... I wasn't. That's when he gave me the Confidence Hat! He said that it was magical and would give me the confidence to stand up for myself the next time those kids bullied me. So, I put it on, and guess what happened?"

"Nothing?" Jordan guesses.

"Wrong," Jace says, "I put it on, and I could feel the confidence streaming through me. Pinky said I was practically radiating!"

Matias furrows his brow. "Are humans supposed to radiate?"

"And then, when Jessica and her crew came back, Pinky jumped into my locker, and I made sure my hat was on tight. Jessica said, 'Hey, look, Jace is wearing his I can't read hat.' But this time, when they all laughed, I laughed the hardest of all."

Jace's friends are riveted as he continues. "Wearing the hat made me remember what I'm best at. So I said, 'Want to know what's really funny, Jessica? I may need extra help with reading, but I don't need any extra help with this...' And then with the help of Pinkie's magic, my cello suddenly appeared!"

"Okay, that's kind of cool," Jordan says. "What happened?"

"I started playing," Jace says, "And I was AMAZING! I played this Bach piece that I've been struggling with, and I swear I saw a tear in Jessica's eye as the last notes faded. She said it was the most beautiful song she'd ever heard. All thanks to my Confidence Hat."

Hudson leans close to get a better look at the sparkly pink hat. "Uh, Jace? Did you read the tag?"

"What tag?" Jace asks, taking off the hat to examine it. He reads the tag aloud. *"ATTENTION: THE CONFIDENCE HAT DOES NOT ACTUALLY GIVE YOU CONFIDENCE. THE CONFIDENCE IS WITHIN YOU."*

"Whoa," Matias says. "That's why you could play the cello so well. Because you believed you could do it."

Jordan laughs. "You're asking about the cello? What about the gremlin! Jace, come on, you made all that up, right?"

Jace shrugs, "I guess you'll never know!" He walks off with a wide grin on his face.

ACTIVITY OVERVIEW
Activity 1: Strengths Bingo

OBJECTIVE
Students will explore their strengths and learn that we all have reasons to be confident. They will learn that they can combine their strengths with others to accomplish their goals.

MATERIALS
- ✓ Strengths Bingo (pre-filled card) or My Own Strengths Bingo (blank card) (downloadable PDFs)
- ✓ Crayons or markers

PROMPT
We all have our own unique strengths. Today, we are going to discover what those strengths are by playing a special game of Bingo to explore not just our own strengths, but those of our classmates.

PROCEDURE
- The goal of this game is for students to fill in every square of their Bingo card with either their own strength or the strength of a classmate.
- Choose your preferred Bingo card format. Both pre-filled and blank Bingo cards are included in the downloadable PDF file. If you are creating your own cards by filling in the Blank Bingo Sheet, make sure that each student has at least five strengths they can identify with.
- Hand out a Bingo card to each student. Students read through the Bingo card and color in the star symbol on each box that they think describes them.
- All students walk around to find a partner who has marked each of the squares they need to complete their pattern. They can color in the smiley face when they find someone who has starred the box they need. The first student to complete the card calls BINGO.
- Depending on group size, you may set a rule that a student can only use one response from each class member so that all kids are participating equitably.

Modification
Set students up for success by adjusting the number of boxes they need to find a match for.

Students can fill in a pattern like an X, a checkerboard, or even a diamond shape.

Younger students may call out BINGO once they have found a certain number of matches on their card.

CLOSURE
Closing discussion questions:
- What would have happened in our game if everyone had listed the same strengths?
- What strengths of yours can be added to the Bingo card?

Copyright © SuperDville

CHAPTER 7: Confidence | ACTIVITY 1: Strengths Bingo

Strengths Bingo

Name: _____ Date: _____

	B	I	N	G	O
1	☆ ☺ Speaking Languages	☆ ☺ Being Kind	☆ ☺ Dancing	☆ ☺ Gymnastics	☆ ☺ Riding Bikes
2	☆ ☺ Making People Laugh	☆ ☺ Reading	☆ ☺ Doing puzzles	☆ ☺ Trying New Things	☆ ☺ Sports
3	☆ ☺ Writing	☆ ☺ Swimming	☆ ☺ Taking care of animals	☆ ☺ Knowing Song Lyrics	☆ ☺ Playing Cards
4	☆ ☺ Telling Stories	☆ ☺ Building Legos	☆ ☺ Being a Good Listener	☆ ☺ Math Facts	☆ ☺ Playing Pretend
5	☆ ☺ Baking	☆ ☺ Gaming	☆ ☺ Skating	☆ ☺ Drawing	☆ ☺ Making Friends

CHAPTER 7: Confidence | ACTIVITY 1: Strengths Bingo

My Own Strengths Bingo

Name: _____ Date: _____

	B	I	N	G	O
1	☆ ☺	☆ ☺	☆ ☺	☆ ☺	☆ ☺
2	☆ ☺	☆ ☺	☆ ☺	☆ ☺	☆ ☺
3	☆ ☺	☆ ☺	☆ ☺	☆ ☺	☆ ☺
4	☆ ☺	☆ ☺	☆ ☺	☆ ☺	☆ ☺
5	☆ ☺	☆ ☺	☆ ☺	☆ ☺	☆ ☺

Copyright © SuperDville   The Teacher's Toolbox For Every Child

ACTIVITY OVERVIEW
Activity 2: Best Friend Voice

OBJECTIVE
Students will practice talking to themselves with the kindness they would show to a friend.

MATERIALS
✓ Self-Talk Matching Game (downloadable PDF)

PROMPT

As we go about our day, our thinking brain talks us through our choices. Some people hear this as words in their heads—this is called self-talk.

This voice can help us feel good about ourselves and encourage us, like a good friend would. But it can also make us feel bad about ourselves and stop us from feeling confident, the way a bully would.

The good news is that we can direct this voice by noticing what it is saying, intentionally changing our self-talk, and making more positive choices about what and how we think.

Today, we will play the Self-Talk Matching Game to practice transforming "bullying self-talk" into "best friend self-talk" by thinking about what we would tell a good friend who needed help.

PROCEDURE
- Have the students complete the Self-Talk Matching Game in pairs or small groups.
- When finished, bring the group together and share the sample scenario below. Brainstorm as a class some things Joey's best friend voice might say in this situation:
  - Joey worked hard on his science fair project. When he showed his poster to Dylan on the bus, Dylan barely looked at it and started talking about a video game instead.

CLOSURE

Review the answers to the matching chart as a class. Discuss why groups chose their answers.

Closing discussion question:
- Can you think of any other best friend voice phrases?

96 Chapter: 7 Confidence

CHAPTER 7: Confidence | ACTIVITY 2: Best Friend Voice
Self-Talk Matching Game

Name: _____ Date: _____

Choose the phrase from the best friend phrase bank that could replace the inner bully voice. Write the letter in the box.

Bully Voice Phrase Bank	
1. I'm too slow. Why can't I hurry up?	
2. Everyone saw me fail.	
3. I'm so dumb. I can't believe I got that question wrong!	
4. I'm so bad at this. Why even try?	
5. No one even likes me.	
6. They're all gossiping about me.	

Best Friend Voice Phrase Bank	
a. I've got this. I just have to take my time.	**d.** I think I'm cool no matter what they think.
b. I like me no matter what anyone else thinks.	**e.** It's OK that I'm not good at this yet—I know I'll get better if I keep trying!
c. Getting a question wrong doesn't mean I'm dumb. It means I'm learning.	**f.** No one is paying attention to what I'm doing. I won't give up!

ACTIVITY OVERVIEW
Activity 3: Comfort Zone Challenge

OBJECTIVE
Students will build confidence by identifying ways they regularly challenge themselves with activities in their Stretch Zone.

MATERIALS
- ✓ Zones of Challenge (downloadable PDF)
- ✓ Writing tools

PROMPT

Today, we will be talking about the three zones of challenge: the Comfort Zone, the Stress Zone, and the Stretch Zone.

Our Comfort Zone is where we feel things are easy, relaxing, or even boring for us to do.

The opposite of our Comfort Zone is our Stress Zone. Activities in the Stress Zone can feel challenging, overwhelming, and even a little scary. This is what we experience when what we need to do seems impossible, and we feel overwhelmed.

The Stretch Zone is a sweet spot between the Comfort Zone and the Stress Zone. In this zone, we feel engaged, excited, capable, and like we can overcome challenges. Activities in our Stretch Zone help us discover what we are capable of! When trying things in our Stretch Zone, we often realize that facing difficult things reminds us how strong we are!

PROCEDURE

- As a class, brainstorm examples to identify activities in the Comfort and Stress Zone. Start with extreme examples to help them grasp the idea. For example, "putting on socks" and "climbing Mount Everest." Point out that each person's Stretch Zone will be different.

- Then, go through the below chart, prompting students to place each example on their own worksheet in the zone where it belongs for them:

| Math homework | Painting | Doing a cartwheel |
| Singing in front of others | Reading chapter books | Playing basketball |

- Next, challenge students to independently think of at least three Stretch Zone activities they do regularly and one they'd like to try but are nervous about.

- Encourage them to use words or pictures to represent each activity.

CLOSURE

Invite volunteers to share one of their Stretch Zone activities. Prompt them to highlight the activity they are most excited to try.

Chapter: 7 Confidence

CHAPTER 7: Confidence | ACTIVITY 3: Comfort Zone Challenge

Zones of Challenge

Name: _____ Date: _____

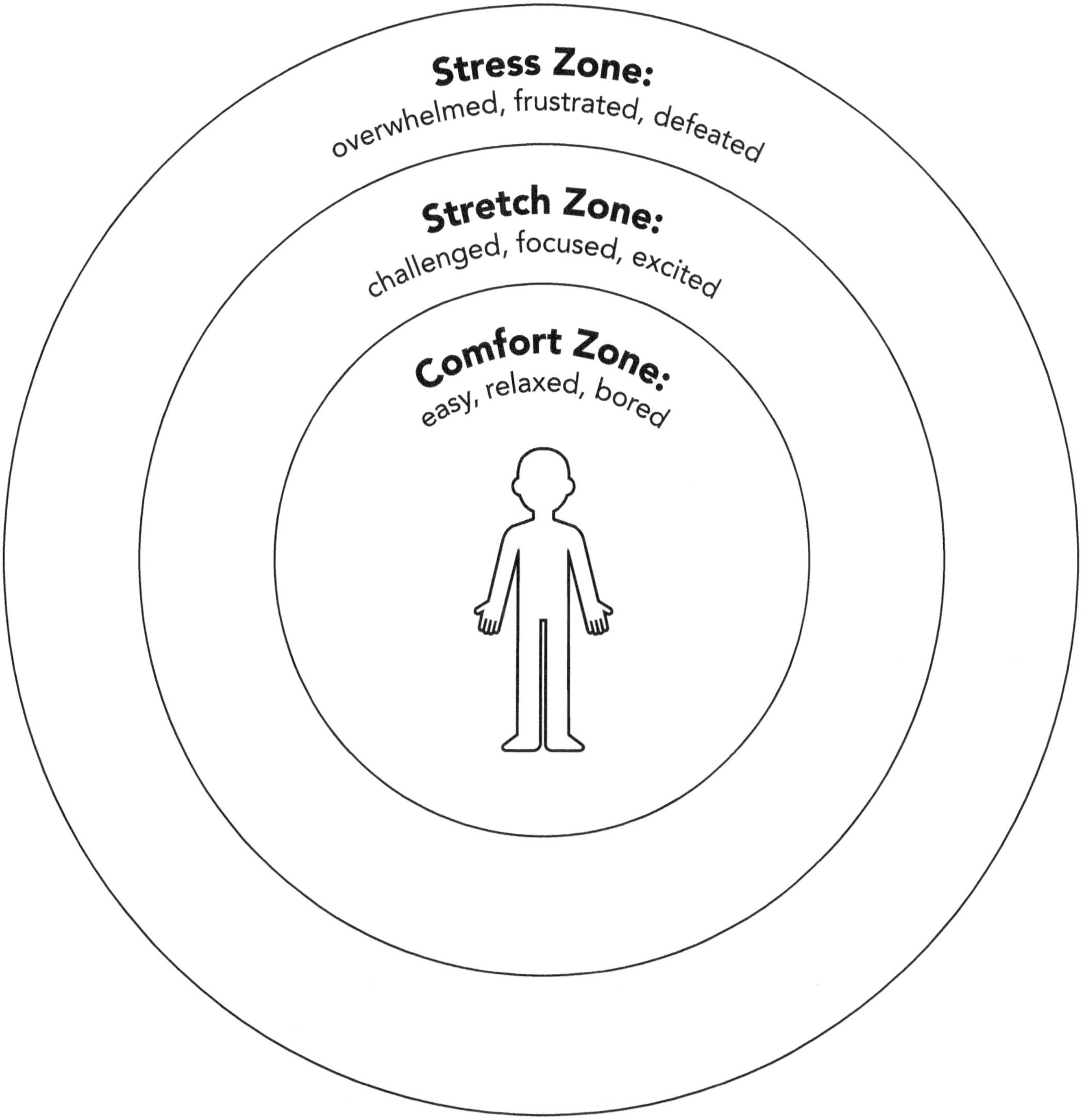

Stress Zone:
overwhelmed, frustrated, defeated

Stretch Zone:
challenged, focused, excited

Comfort Zone:
easy, relaxed, bored

ACTIVITY OVERVIEW
Activity 4: Listening Circle

OBJECTIVE
Students will reflect on the bullying Jace experienced in the story and strategize together about ways to respond to bullying in their community.

NOTE
While many anti-bullying lessons focus on prevention, the sad reality is that having a disability is a risk factor for bullying (UNESCO, 2021). Prior to engaging in this activity, teachers should be cognizant that some students will likely have personal experiences with bullying. They may elect to conduct guidance, we suggest reading through Pacer.org/bullying for talking to kids about bullying.

MATERIALS
NA

PROMPT
In the story, Jace is bullied because he has dyslexia and is still learning to read. Even though we all learn at different paces, and all speeds are okay, Jace is still sad and embarrassed when Jessica jokes about him being in Special Ed.

Today, we will have a listening circle to help us brainstorm how to respond if we see or experience bullying. This is an important conversation, so we have rules for our circle to help make sure everyone can speak and be heard.

PROCEDURE
- Write the rules on the board and review them as a group. Students may add rules they wish to include.
- **Listening Circle Rules**
    - No "shoulding," fixes, or forcing positivity. Ex. You should just get over it!
    - What is said in the listening circle stays in the listening circle.
    - No talking during other shares. Listen without planning what you want to say.
    - Pass if you choose to. When you wish to share, ask for a turn.
- **Reread the excerpt from the story below:**
  It happened after school, right after band practice. I was just about to open my locker and put my cello away when Jessica and her posse stopped me. And Jessica says, 'Hey Jace, did you learn to read today in Special Ed?' And then she and her friends high-fived each other like it was the funniest joke ever."
- **Ask these questions, allowing each student in the circle to respond or pass.**
    - How would you feel if you saw this happen?
    - What would you want Jace to know if you could talk to him right after Jessica walked away?
    - What would you do next if this happened to you? What would you do if you saw it happen to someone else?

CLOSURE
Thank students for their bravery in speaking openly about bullying. Note any students who want to talk more and follow up with them later.

ACTIVITY OVERVIEW
Extension Activities

EXTENSION 1:
Create Your Own Strengths Bingo Card

Ask students to use the blank Bingo card to create their own set of strengths and characteristics. Challenge them to include:

- 5 character traits – Example: kind, funny
- 5 skills – Example: Can ride a bike
- 5 likes or loves – Example: Likes Gummy Worms
- 5 interests or curiosities – Example: Interested in outer space
- 5 traits of their choosing

EXTENSION 2:
Stretch Zone Challenge

Have students plan to try one of their stretch zone activities. Have them record their feelings immediately afterward with a drawing, a voice or video recording, or in writing.

- What was the scariest part of trying something new?
- How did you feel before, during, and after completing the activity?
- What were you able to do that you didn't expect?

Print Stretch Zone Challenge Sheet printable from the downloadable PDF file.

IDEAS & NOTES

_____
_____
_____
_____
_____
_____
_____
_____
_____

CHAPTER 7: Confidence | EXTENSION 2: Stretch Zone Challenge

Stretch Zone Challenge Sheet

Name: _____ Date: _____

My Challenge Activity:

How I felt before trying my challenge activity:	How I felt after trying my challenge activity:

Next time I do my challenge activity I will feel:

Chapter 8:
Self-Advocacy

Discussion Guide

READ ALOUD OBJECTIVE
Students will consider the ways of learning that work best for them. They will also reflect on how to be honest and unapologetic about their needs.

STORY SUMMARY
Ayana is embarrassed to tell her classmates that she goes to the Resource Room. Her friends share their strategies for talking to other students about getting help at school. Kaia describes how she uses magic mind tricks to hide that she goes to the Resource Room. Hudson explains that he is honest about the support he gets; in fact, he even uses fancy words to talk about it. Charlie shares that she just tells the truth when kids ask.

READ ALOUD INTRODUCTION
At school, each of us has a different way of learning. The best learning methods for some students include working in small groups, getting in extra practice, and doing hands-on projects. In the story, the main characters get extra help in a part of their school called the Resource Room. While we read, think about some of the things that help you to learn the best.

READ ALOUD CLOSURE
In the story, Ayana felt she couldn't be honest about going to the resource room to help with her learning. She knew that going there was important and helpful to her, but she found it hard to say that to her classmates. In this chapter, we will be learning about self-advocacy, or how we stick up for ourselves to ensure our needs are met.

LISTEN TO THE AUDIO VERSION OF THE STORY

COMPREHENSION QUESTIONS

1. **What is the Resource Room?**
   Answer: The Resource Room is a place in a school where kids can get help with their schoolwork or take extra time to practice challenging skills.

2. **Why did Ayana hide her visits to the Resource Room?**
   Answer: Ayana feared what her friends would think if they knew she needed extra help at school.

3. **Why did Hudson use so many fancy words to tell his friends he went to the Resource Room?**
   Answer: Hudson thought that making the resource room sound like a high-tech laboratory would impress his friends instead of making them judgmental.

DISCUSSION QUESTIONS

1. Why do the students feel nervous about telling their friends they have to go to another room for extra help?

2. Do you think Kaia's strategy of using magical mind tricks or Charlie's strategy of being honest but making the truth sound fancy is better? Why?

3. What do you think Ayana should do? Why?

104   Chapter: 8 Self-Advocacy

READ ALOUD:
Resource Room

Hudson, Charlie, and Kaia are playing cards in the rec room when Ayana comes in, her shoulders sagging and an upset look on her face.

Hudson notices her sad expression. "What's up Ayana?" he says, looking at her over his hand of cards, "Are you okay?"

Ayana looks shy for a moment and doesn't speak up. She just plops down on a beanbag.

"You can tell us," Hudson says, "We're your friends!"

Ayana sighs. "You know how my mom and I met with my teacher to ask about getting me extra help with staying organized?"

"Yeah," Charlie says, "I thought that was super brave of you to ask for help."

"I guess," Ayana says, "but to get the extra help, I have to leave class and go to the Resource Room a few days a week. And whenever I get back from the Resource Room, someone from my class always asks me where I've been. I never know what to say. It makes me wish I never asked for help in the first place."

"That used to happen to me when I first started going to the Resource Room," Charlie tells her. "Having a learning difference makes me feel different enough without having to explain why I go to a different classroom."

Hudson nods. "It's tough to tell your friends where you are, especially if you feel nervous or embarrassed about it."

Kaia pipes up on the other side of the table. "I find it's best to use magical mind tricks."

"Magical mind tricks?" Ayana asks, laughing. "Really?"

"Yes!" Kaia says, smiling mischievously. "When I come back from the Resource Room, I hide under a big black cloak," Kaia wiggles her fingers at Ayana, "and then I try to hypnotize them!"

"You do not!" Hudson laughs.

"Okay, maybe not," Kaia says, her eyes sparkling. "But I just give the most boring answer I can, like *Oh I had to alphabetize my erasers*. I basically hypnotize them out of being interested."

Charlie laughs. "That's pretty funny, Kaia," she says, "I just tell the truth: I go there for help with my handwriting. It's easier for me to practice if I'm not rushing to take notes

continued next page

Chapter 8 Activities

Activity: **Self-Advocacy Role Play**
Activity Type: Role-Play

Activity 2: **Megaphone Activity**
Activity Type: Art Project

Activity 3: **Your Perfect Learning Space**
Activity Type: Design Challenge

Activity 4: **Super D! Letters**
Activity Type: Discussion

Extension 1: **Dear Teacher**
Activity Type: Writing

Extension 2: **Self-Advocacy Comic Strip**
Activity Type: Art

SEL Vocabulary

resource room [noun]: this is a place in some schools where students can get extra help

self-advocacy [noun]: using your words and actions to stick up for your needs

Resource Room
continued

in class. Plus, I'm all about hanging with the occupational therapist, Ms. Coleman."

"Yeah," Hudson says. "When I come back from the Resource Room and people ask me where I've been, I tell them where I was and what I did."

"Just tell them the truth…" Ayana murmurs, considering.

"Right," Hudson continues, "I say I was aided by a team of highly trained cognitive professionals, and we analyzed how my brain processes words and computes numbers. Then we figured out a way I could function at the highest level of intelligence."

"Whoa," Kaia says, impressed. "You made the Resource Room sound like a high-tech laboratory!"

Hudson laughs. "Well, it kind of is! I mean, it has tables and bean bags and teachers instead of test tubes and mad scientists, but it's a place where we figure things out, just like a laboratory."

Ayana thinks for a moment and then breaks into a wide smile. "I know just what to say when people ask me about it!"

The next day, when Ayana comes back to class after her time in the Resource Room, everyone asks where she's been.

"Oh," Ayana says lightly, "I asked for extra help because I was having trouble staying organized. I was in the Resource Room, organizing my books and papers to create a masterful system that maximizes efficiency and increases productivity. What did you all do while I was gone?"

She grins at their impressed reactions and can't wait to share with Kaia, Hudson, and Charlie.

ACTIVITY OVERVIEW
Activity 1: Self-Advocacy Role Play

OBJECTIVE
Students will practice speaking up about their wants and needs. They will learn some useful phrases that they can use in the future.

MATERIALS
✓ Self-Advocacy Scenario Cards (downloadable PDF)

✓ Self-Advocacy Sentence Starters (downloadable PDF)

PROMPT

Sometimes, when we need something, it can be hard to figure out the best way to ask for it. For example, I will ask for a snack two different ways, and I want you to tell me what you notice.

"Could I please have a snack? I'm so hungry I can't really focus."

"Hey, give me that cookie!"

The first way is polite and includes a reason why I am asking. The second way is demanding and impolite.

Today, we will be actors and practice making requests.

PROCEDURE
- Break students into pairs and give each a scenario from the Self-Advocacy Scenario Cards. One student will be the self-advocate, and one student will be either a teacher or a friend. Tell them that whoever is playing the teacher or friend role has to decide whether they would agree to the request.
- Have the students take turns acting the scenario so each student has a chance to play both roles.
- Hand out the Self-Advocacy Sentence Starters sheet and have the kids repeat the role play, choosing one sentence starter to try out.

CLOSURE
Closing discussion questions:
- What were some of the best strategies for making these requests? What didn't work?
  - Key points: Being polite rather than demanding, explaining reasons for requests, and listening to the partner's point of view help.
- Which was your favorite sentence starter? What did you like about it?

CHAPTER 8: Self-Advocacy | ACTIVITY 1: Self Advocacy Role Play

Self-Advocacy Scenario Cards

Cut the cards apart along the dotted lines.

✂ —

Scenario 1   **Roles:** Self-Advocate and Teacher

In language arts class, the teacher is explaining persuasive writing. They are going through the lesson fast, and the Self-Advocate is lost.

What could the Self-Advocate say?

— —

Scenario 2   **Roles:** Self-Advocate and Teacher

The teacher had the Self-Advocate stay in during recess to finish an assignment they didn't have time to finish during class. The worksheet is super long, and the Self-Advocate needs a break.

What could the Self-Advocate say?

— —

Scenario 3   **Roles:** Self-Advocate and Friend

The Self-Advocate is working on a group project for science class with a friend. The friend wants to do a project about horses, but the Self-Advocate doesn't like that topic. The Self-Advocate doesn't want to hurt the friend's feelings, but also wants to pick a topic that they both like.

What could the Self-Advocate say?

— —

Scenario 4   **Roles:** Self-Advocate and Friend

The Self-Advocate's friend keeps calling them a silly nickname. It makes the Self-Advocate feel embarrassed. The Self-Advocate has tried to show the friend playfully that the name makes them feel bad, but the friend isn't getting the message.

What could the Self-Advocate say?

— —

CHAPTER 8: Self-Advocacy | ACTIVITY 1: Self Advocacy Role Play

Self-Advocacy Sentence Starters

- I'm having a hard time with...
- I need ...
- Can we please ...?
- It would be really helpful to me because...
- This is making me feel ...
- I don't like it when...
- Could we try ...
- Could you please help me by...?

ACTIVITY OVERVIEW
Activity 2: Megaphone Activity

OBJECTIVE
In this art activity, students will practice identifying and advocating for the support they need to learn.

This activity is designed to get students thinking about their needs in different academic situations and empower them to ask for what they need.

MATERIALS
- ✓ Megaphone Cutout (downloadable PDF)
- ✓ Needs Word Bank (downloadable PDF)
- ✓ Scissors
- ✓ Tape
- ✓ Writing, coloring supplies

PROMPT
What do you need to be ready to learn at home or at school? Everyone has different needs, and those needs usually fall into three categories.

There are supplies, like if you need a pencil gripper or fidget toy. There are also environmental needs, for example, if you need to be seated close to the teacher to help you focus. And there are body needs, like if you need a break to move your body or if you are hungry.

It's important to know what you need to learn, and it's also important to know how to ask for what you need.

Today, we are going to create megaphones! You have seen them—people use them to make sure their voice is heard loud and clear. Today we'll use them to raise our voices about our needs for learning.

PROCEDURE
- Give each student a Megaphone Cutout and a copy of the Needs Word Bank, a blank piece of paper (or let them choose their own if you're using construction paper), along with writing and coloring supplies.
- Have students use the word bank to get their ideas going as they consider the following questions below—or come up with your own—and ask them to circle their answers on the Needs Word Bank handout.
  - What kind of supplies help you do your best work? This could be things like a wobble stool, fidget spinner, or headphones.
  - What kind of environment is your favorite to work in? Some kids like it really quiet, and some kids like it best when there's some background noise.
  - What do you need to be ready to learn? Do you need frequent breaks to get up and move? Do you need to make sure you get enough sleep?
- Once students have circled their answers, it's time to be creative! Have students use the art supplies to write or draw their answers on their megaphones before cutting them out and taping them into finished cones.

CLOSURE
When they are done decorating, break students into small groups. Have the take turns using their megaphones to share what their specific needs are.

110   Chapter: 8 Self-Advocacy

CHAPTER 8: Self-Advocacy | ACTIVITY 2: Megaphone Activity
Megaphone Cutout

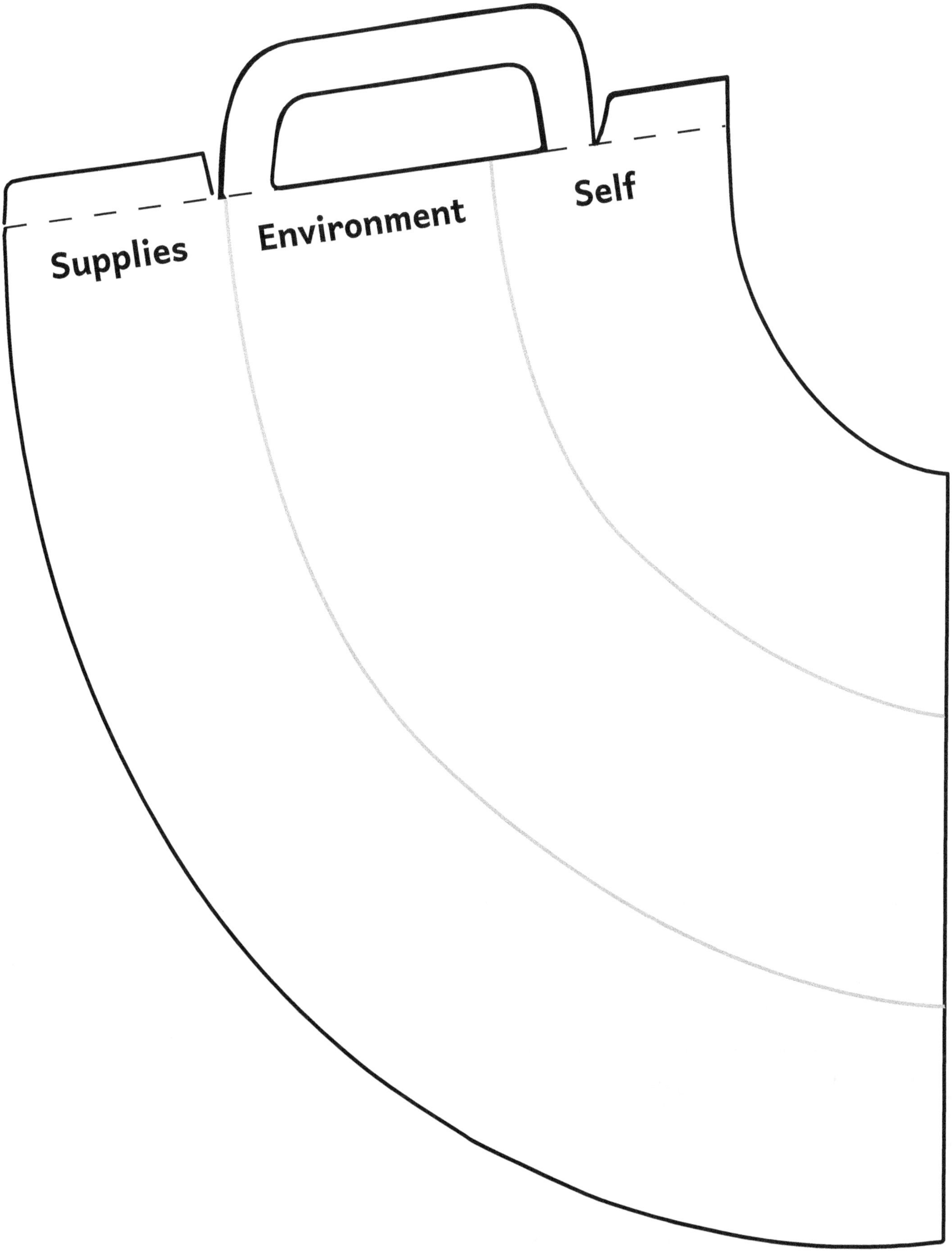

Supplies

Environment

Self

Copyright © SuperDville

The Teacher's Toolbox For Every Child   **111**

CHAPTER 8: Confidence | ACTIVITY 2: Megaphone Activity

Needs Word Bank

Supplies			
Pencil	Paper	Scissors	My folder
Crayons	A coat	My lunchbox	A fidget
What other ideas can you think of?			

Environment			
Quiet	Somewhere I can focus	A clear spot on my desk	A trash can to throw away my scraps
Room to move	Lights off	A reading lamp	A cozy place to sit
What other ideas can you think of?			

Self			
Snack	Water	Rest	Movement
Take a break	A timer	Directions explained out loud	Talk through questions
What other ideas can you think of?			

ACTIVITY OVERVIEW
Activity 3: Your Perfect Learning Space

OBJECTIVE
Students will identify challenges in their learning environments and imagine solutions to these issues. This exercise is designed for the students to feel a sense of agency at school.

To help students advocate for their learning needs, we can start by encouraging them to envision their own solutions. In this activity, kids will imagine their ideal learning environment. They should be validated and encouraged to include both realistic and fantastical ideas and solutions.

MATERIALS
- ✓ Students can select drawing materials, magazines or photos for collaging, clay, or even building materials

PROMPT
Today, we will imagine what the perfect learning environment designed just for you would be like. Take a moment to look around the room. What are some of your favorite things about our class? You can think about parts of the room, special objects, decorations, or tools. Now, think about what parts of the classroom you would change if you got to be in charge of designing this space.

PROCEDURE
- Write the following question prompts on the board:
    - How would the perfect learning environment for your learning needs look, sound, smell, and feel?
    - In our classroom, what doesn't work well for you and how would you try to solve it in your design?
- Invite students to draw, build, or write about their perfect classroom. Give them at least 15 minutes to work independently.

CLOSURE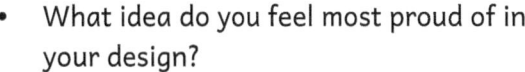

Invite students to share their designs.

Closing discussion questions:

- What idea do you feel most proud of in your design?
- Did you notice any patterns in the challenges or solutions the group came up with?
- Were there any solutions that you think we could bring into our classroom in real life?

The Teacher's Toolbox For Every Child 113

ACTIVITY OVERVIEW
Activity 4: Super D! Letters

OBJECTIVE
Students will read letters from the Super D! Kids that model how to talk openly about their learning differences using positive, strength-based language.

MATERIALS
✓ Super D! Letters - (downloadable PDF)

✓ My Super D! Letter - (downloadable PDF)

PROMPT
Did you know that all the kids in the Super D! after school program have learning differences like dyslexia, dyscalculia, or ADHD? Today, we will read letters from some Super D! Kids, sharing their experiences with learning differences.

While we read these letters from the Super D! Kids, notice how they describe their learning differences.

PROCEDURE
- Read the Super D! Letters as a group. Teachers can read them to the group while students follow along, or a student volunteer can read.
- Discuss each follow-up question as a class.
- Ask students to write their own Super D! Letter. Some questions to get them thinking are:
  - What do you know about the ways that you think and learn best?
  - What tips do you have for other kids about advocating for themselves at school?

CLOSURE
When the group has finished their letters, ask if anyone would like to share.

Closing discussion questions:
- What in the letters made you curious?
- Was their anything one of your classmates shared that you related to?

CHAPTER 8: Self-Advocacy | ACTIVITY 4: Super D! Letters

Super D! Letters: Ellie

Hi,

My name is Ellie. I'm nine years old, and I have dyslexia.

I don't know about you, but it took me a while to learn how to speak up for myself. Now, when I feel overwhelmed or behind, I take a deep breath and then immediately ask for help from someone. I know all kids can feel overwhelmed when they need support, but kids like me with dyslexia can really feel this way a lot.

I was not always good at speaking up. The first time I tried telling someone I needed help was with my swim team coach. We were doing something in practice called intervals. He said that I needed to add and subtract seconds really fast in my head. I was so confused, and I realized I had better let him know or I was going to mess things up badly! I told him that I have dyslexia and that what he was asking for was really hard for me. At first, he said, "Doesn't that mean you read upside down?" It was frustrating that he didn't get it and tried to make it a joke, but when I explained that it just takes me longer to process certain things in my brain he understood why intervals were so difficult and helped me by coming up with an easier counting method.

How about you? Have you ever had to ask for help? What happened?

From,
Ellie

CHAPTER 8: Self-Advocacy | ACTIVITY 4: Super D! Letters

Super D! Letters: Ari

Hi,

I'm Ari and I thought I would write to you about my ADHD. If you have ADHD you will probably relate to what I am saying, and if you don't you will probably understand more about ADHD after you read this letter.

Often I'm happy with my ADHD because it helps me come up with great ideas. Seriously, my ADHD helps me think about a lot of different things—sometimes all at once. It's like being on a rollercoaster in my brain. It's an exciting adventure each day. It takes me zooming up, down, and in a million directions. The point is that my brain takes me to a lot of places that I can't even imagine. A rollercoaster can be fun and also surprising. It's the same with ADHD. You know, it's scary that while in math class, I'm thinking about why a rabbit's foot is supposed to be lucky. Or, while I'm playing video games with my brother, I might suddenly realize, "Hey, I just figured out the answer to that math problem."

Anyways, my tip to you is love your brain. Love the rollercoaster ride it brings you on!

What do you love about your brain?

How would you describe it? Is it like a roller coaster or something else? A microscope? A computer?

From,
Ari

CHAPTER 8: Self-Advocacy | ACTIVITY 4: Super D! Letters

My Super D! Letter

ACTIVITY OVERVIEW
Extension Activities

EXTENSION 1:
Dear Teacher

What do you wish your teacher knew about how you learn? Write a letter to your teacher describing the things that help you to learn best. Be sure to answer the questions below:

- What was the best time you have ever had learning something new in class? What made it so fun or engaging?
- What classroom activities do you wish there were more of at school? (art projects, games, read-aloud, etc.)
- What topics or areas do you feel most excited to learn about?

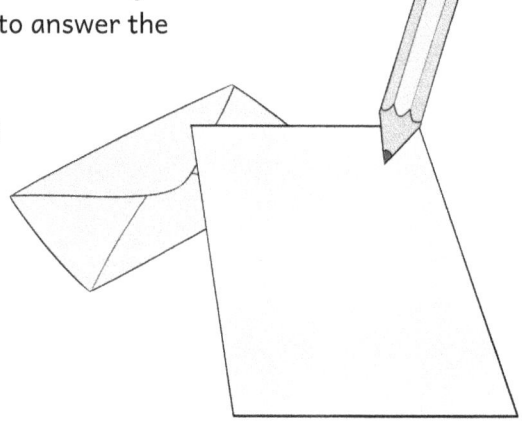

EXTENSION 2:
Self-Advocacy Comic Strip

Print Self-Advocacy Comic Strip printable from the downloadable PDF file.

Using the Self-Advocacy Comic Strip frame, have students create a 1-2 page scene to show an example of self-advocacy for their peers. Their comic should include:

- A character in a situation where it's tricky to speak up for themselves.
- The character demonstrating one strategy for self-advocacy.
- The outcome of the strategy—did it work? Why or why not?

IDEAS & NOTES

_____
_____
_____
_____
_____
_____
_____

CHAPTER 8: Self-Advocacy | EXTENSION ACTIVITY 2: Self-Advocacy Comic Strip

Self-Advocacy Comic Strip

Name: _____   Date: _____

Where different learners make a difference!

At SuperDville, we believe that all children, regardless of how they learn, deserve to experience the personal growth, encouragement, and support that can come from focusing on their strengths. ***The Teacher's Toolbox for Every Child*** comes out of our commitment to provide resources that will further SuperDville's mission.

Similar to the read-alouds at the beginning of each chapter, you will find 5-minute episodes on our website, all of which are also available in Spanish! The activities in this book are extensions of themes explored in the SuperDville curriculum, but the format of a book allows us to expand and give you more detailed and enriched content.

Your students will enjoy watching the episodes, which will deepen their understanding of each theme. (You can find free samples to watch on the home page at SuperDville.com). All of the kid actors in the episodes are children with learning differences in real life. Therefore, SuperDville creates a powerful peer-to-peer experience for students who have a learning difference, helping them feel connected, accepted, and not alone. In turn, students who are not struggling learners develop empathy and learn how to be part of a community where all skill sets are embraced and supported.

We hope that this book will be a resource that you use for years to come in your classrooms, after-school programs, resource rooms and beyond. Subscribe to SuperDville.com and use the videos hand in hand with the book. Together you will have two powerful new tools in your toolbox that will be beneficial for ALL children.

SuperDville is a community; you can sign-up for our newsletter, read bi-monthly blogs and join the user-only Facebook group.

Please go to SuperDville.com or use the QR code below to subscribe.

www.ingramcontent.com/pod-product-compliance
Lightning Source LLC
Chambersburg PA
CBHW080747300426
44114CB00019B/2665